Living a Good Life

Moral Literacy for Young People

Living a Good Life

Moral Literacy for Young People

Ranjit Powar
and
Pramod Rai

www.thebrowser.org
Publishers & Booksellers

First Published in India by **The Browser** 2021
(An imprint of J.G.S. Enterprises Pvt. Ltd.)
SCO 14-15, Sector 8-C, Chandigarh 160 009
Email: service@thebrowser.org

ISBN 978-93-88150-13-2

www.thebrowser.org

CONTENTS

Preface

I have often counseled parents distressed over a lack of values and self-discipline in their teenage children. "Where did we go wrong?" they ask. I believe that child-rearing practices are only part of the problem, with myriad factors including biological, social, political, and environmental contributions to undisciplined and amoral behavior in teenagers. The human brain is in the process of continuous development up till age 20. Therefore, teenagers are biologically unable to exercise moral reasoning like adults or fathom the long-term effects of bad decisions and amoral behavior.

The world is on a roller-coaster ride like never before, with both adults and youngsters scrambling to prove one's abilities in a challenging scenario. Students realize that their academic achievements and preparation for a brilliant, paying career define their young lives. The important thing is to reach there by hook or crook, with moral issues taking a back seat. The message conveyed by their parents and teachers is that the goal justifies the means.

Teachers are in a rush to finish the exhaustive syllabi and ensure good results, while parents push their children to do what it takes to jump higher to clear high bars, like a horse in an obstacle race. Who has the time for ethics or values?

Belief in institutionalized religion has been reduced mainly to observing festivals and mechanical traditions with no attention to understanding or applying its intrinsic values. Unfortunately, it is more often used as an assertion of identity and political tool than a moral guide. Many self-styled godmen and god women have further undermined religious piety through their illegal and immoral activities. Highly restrictive and restraining to fit in a multi-cultural world on the move, religion fails to inspire devotion in many skeptical modern youngsters, who need to rationalize beliefs instead of following them blindly.

Where does a youngster turn to find an inspiring role model? Society is not devoid of moral people, but they are not projected as much as the 'successful' ones. What teenagers end up watching on the television, internet, and cinema are glamorous actors, corrupt politicians, and business tycoons. They listen to music that glorifies violence and sex, access pornography on the internet, and learn that their favorite film star consumes *ganja*. Politicians grab power through foul means and come with criminal histories. Their agenda is not to serve the country but to stay in power, make money, and divide people based on caste and religion. Bureaucrats, judiciary, and police indulge in high-handedness and corruption instead of delivering good administration and justice. India has emerged as one of the most unsafe countries for women who are constantly exposed to harassment, molestation, and rape. Gender discrimination continues to target women and LGBTQ members in all walks of life.

Despite being in the 21st century, we are still eons away from ensuring equality, fraternity, financial security, and individual freedom to a large population. Education and health care remain unavailable for many. Our environment is being degraded each year, endangering animal species and fouling the earth, air, and water for humans. It is time to soul search and understand where we are going wrong. There can be no wholesome progress of a society or nation without a strong moral and ethical fiber. Education is incomplete without including a sense of moral values to ensure that it benefits humanity and not for selfish and corrupt ends. Scoring high marks in science and humanities is appreciable, but growing up with a clear sense of values to ensure a fair, compassionate, and just society is of utmost importance. I hope this book can offer an ethical code to teenagers that convinces them to imbibe moral values through reasoning, and not because anyone says so.

Ranjit Powar

1

Does the World Need Ethics?

> To educate a person in mind and not morals is to educate a menace to society.
> —Theodore Roosevelt

Ah! It feels good to be young, living on a young planet in a young solar system, in a universe billions of years old. Eight billion earthlings, a full quarter of you between the ages 10 to 24—your thoughts and ideas will shape the world; you will drive social change and progress; yours will be the crucial decisions to take as you mature. On your shoulders will stand a humane and ethical world.

But that won't come easy; it didn't come easy for your parents, it never has for any generation throughout history. Onwards into your journey to adulthood, you will meet various challenges that will affect your lives for better or worse. As designated drivers of social change and progress, you must acquire not only the knowledge and skills required to lead productive, materially successful lives but also humane and ethical ones.

To go to good academic institutes, have sophisticated laboratories and libraries, and strive towards higher achievement levels is good, but not enough. What differentiates a highly intelligent robot from a human is that humans have a conscience, which the robot does not. More than intelligence, ability, or strength, a developed conscience makes a human superior to robots and other animals. Conscience is nothing but our internalized values, morals, and ethics, which guide our thoughts and actions throughout our lives. It urges us to do the right thing in three ways—it makes us feel that we *ought to do so*; it affords us a feeling of self-approval when we *have done so*; it inflicts a painful feeling of self-reproach when we have *not done so*.

What are Values and Ethics?

Our value systems include our beliefs about right and wrong, what is important to us, and what is not. Ethics are the dos and don'ts adopted by a specific society. Law, religion, community, culture, and family spell out rules about what one may or may not do. The literature we read, the people we admire, and the social media we are exposed to shape our value system. Nevertheless, some finer points are not written anywhere, but instinctively understood and practiced by people with an evolved consciousness. Some ethics issues may be culture-specific and not universal, but basic ethics like truthfulness, honesty, compassion, respect for life and justice are generally universally accepted moral values. They envisage an underlying moral code that guides a person's choices and behavior throughout life.

Have you read the Preamble to the Indian Constitution? It lists some fundamental values and rights for Indian citizens, which must be upheld by the state, law, and individuals. These include sovereignty, socialism, secularism, and democracy, the republican character of the Indian state, justice, liberty, equality, fraternity, human dignity, and unity and integrity of the nation. Since our values are judged in our constitution's perspective, let us understand the meanings of some central terms.

Justice—The idea of a society that gives social, economic, and political justice to all citizens is one of the principles of the Indian Constitution. It means that all persons must have equal opportunities to prosper, be treated as equals in society, and have equal opportunity to participate in political systems through voting or standing for elections.

Liberty—The Preamble prescribes liberty of thought, expression, belief, faith, and worship as one of its core values. These are fundamental rights for people of all communities, religions, and castes.

Equality—All citizens have equal status and opportunity in all avenues, be it education, work, or means to self-fulfilment.

Fraternity—This means promoting a feeling of brotherhood among all people. India has diverse cultures, religions, and communities. They all must co-exist in peace and harmony for the welfare of the nation. Any communal and divisive behavior can cause much damage to the welfare and progress of the country.

Dignity of the Individual—Society is a sum of individuals. The constitution assures upholding the dignity of each individual through respect, concern, and attribution of the rights discussed above. It also includes protecting the individual against physical, sexual, verbal, or mental abuse and allowing full freedom to make one's

choices towards growth and fulfilment.

Why do we Need Values and Ethics?

All of us need a direction to guide our interests, goals, and choices in life. Our ethics and values give us that road map. They affect our choice of friends, social behavior, and relationships. In short, our values are the driving force behind most of our actions. Whenever we face challenges in life and must make crucial decisions, we turn towards our value system to guide us. We can also call them ethics. Society evaluates a person's character, moral standing, and integrity based on his moral values.

We know that if two or more individuals get together to play a simple game, they must abide by the set rules of that game. If any one player refuses to follow the rules, the game cannot go on, and other members will insist on expelling the player. Take the example of a hockey match. To play a successful match, each team must play together by the rules determined for their team and the rules set to play with the opposing team. A referee is appointed to keep a close watch on the team players, ensuring that no player breaks the rules or plays unfairly.

Social groups and societies are like teams that need to have rules and regulations to live together in peace and harmony. The lawmakers and enforcers are the referees here. The persona of the lawmakers has been changing with the evolution of society. In the earliest societies, the village elders or the chief emerged as the lawmaker. The rise of structured religion entrenched it as the ultimate lawgiver. As societies grew more extensive and complex, political bodies came into force, becoming the most powerful regulatory bodies. Politics and religion moved in tandem and acted as the lawgivers. During the long course of social evolution, these rules and regulations became deeply entrenched in the group members' minds. They were internalized in a structured set of dos and don'ts, which came to be termed as morals, ethics, or values.

It is undeniable that human nature tends to be selfish and is all too willing to harm others in one's favor. Remember the story of six-to-twelve-year-old boys marooned on an uninhabited island? In his book *Lord of the Flies*, William Golding explores the human condition and the need for moral consciousness. The boys create their social system, where Ralph is the chosen leader of the group. Rules are decided—keep the fire going, use proper sanitation, obey authority, look after the youngest children, and so on. For a while, these rules of civilized society prevent chaos. As the excitement of liberation from the constraints of the adult world abates, they come face to face with the problems of social existence: filth, competition for power and status, neglect of social responsibility, failure of public policy, and increasing violence. Though some children act wisely and rationally, another group neglects their assigned duties, violates human values, and overthrows the leader. Their uncontrolled lust for excitement, which begins with killing pigs, becomes more savage and ends in thirst for human blood. In such a society, relationships soon break down, as they cannot be sustained without values like loyalty, honesty, and commitment. Ethics is a form of social control that keeps society from falling apart by promoting human relationships, relieving human suffering, resolving conflicts in just ways, and assigning responsibility for actions to create flourishing communities.

The well-being and welfare of our society, families, and individuals depend on how well we all follow ethical rules. The very survival of the human race depends on it. Imagine a society where everyone does whatever they please, disregarding basic moral rules or welfare of others. For example, imagine that Anu promises to help Billi with her assignment the next day provided Billi helps her write her's today. Billi trusts Anu and helps her, but Anu goes for a movie the next day instead of helping Billi. Will Billi feel wronged and angry? What kind of a society will it be where parents neglect and abandon their children; husbands and wives mistrust or cheat each other, and people continuously lie and steal for their profit?

Young people should imbibe a robust value system to grow up as individuals with a sound moral fiber. Such people are happier, have better relationships, and contribute positively to society. Failure to learn ethics leaves them confused and likely to make poor choices, resulting in severe problems for themselves, their families, and society. A person cannot be expected to apply something she has never learned. Thus the need for discussing and learning ethics and values in education.

Youth in the New World

The world has gone through tremendous changes in the last few decades due to rapid advances in technology and biosciences, industrialization, the evolution of democratic political systems, and broader access to information and education. It has brought remarkable changes in lifestyles, modes of livelihood, family structures, relationships, and individual behavior. The world has shrunk to be a global village. Nations, communities, and social groups are no longer self-contained units. People from different cultures and countries influence each other through travel, literature, and social media. When youngsters are exposed to ideas and modes of behavior at odds with their learnings, it leads to confusion and doubt. Which way of life is right? The one their grandparents and parents taught them, or the one they see on American TV?

Religions speak about rules which may have been relevant in the previous century. However, they are challenging to follow in the present time. What is the touchstone for one to base one's decisions and choices?

It is time to evolve and enforce a value system that is in keeping with the lifestyle and challenges we face in today's technological world. Some fundamental human values are timeless and will apply at all times and places. However, there are some social traditions and perspectives we must revaluate for their veracity.

Guidelines for Behaviour

As a youngster, how can you decide between making a good or bad choice? Ask yourself the following questions:

What are my exact reasons for taking this decision?

Am I doing this to take an easy way out of a difficult situation now or because it is the correct thing to do?

Will this decision be fair to others?

Will I admire my friend for doing what I am going to do?

Does this decision damage me or others in any way?

Will it give me only short-term benefit or pleasure, or will it be good for me in the long term?

Am I able to fearlessly disclose this decision to others, or will I need to hide it?

Will I advise my younger sister or brother to do the same?

2

Why be Honest?

Honesty is more than not lying. It is truth-telling, truth-speaking, truth-living, and truth-loving.
—James E. Faust

Honesty is the first virtue extolled by all religions, holy books, and spiritual teachers. Simply put, it means that each of our actions, thoughts and behavior is in keeping with our moral code and the law of the land. Being honest means:

We do not lie to others or mislead them by misrepresenting things.

We do not try to get undue benefits for ourselves at the cost of others who deserve them.

We follow the law at all times.

We do our duty even if no one is watching.

> **We refuse to give in to pressure, threat or money when making a choice.**

Honesty is a tough call. Why should one put oneself through difficult situations when sometimes it is simpler to lie and make things easier for ourselves? There are not many people who can honestly say that they are always honest. Many think that it is acceptable to lie and cheat in small ways to get along small hurdles without being dubbed as dishonest. Are there any good reasons to be honest, even if we think we can get by with little lies? Yes, here are some:

> **Telling a small lie puts us at the risk of being labelled a liar if discovered, damages our reputation, and reduces people's trust in us.**
>
> **One lie often leads to another, which may set off a chain of lies, each more significant than the other.**
>
> **Sometimes the results of a small lie turn out to be much more severe than we imagined.**

Before you decide whether honesty is the best policy or not, remember that not only do the rules of honesty apply to every member of society, they also affect every member for better or worse. The actions of every individual carry a message for others and prompt them to act likewise. If dishonesty becomes the norm, each one of us will be at the receiving end of someone's cheating sometime. Let us look at some real-life situations.

A Bribe for a Right

Nimmi has lost her expensive mobile phone worth twenty-five thousand rupees. She goes to lodge a complaint at the police station, but the cop on duty tries to evade lodging a report because it is a small issue and will create extra work for him. He works long duty hours and feels that he is underpaid by the government. When Nimmi insists on the FIR, he hints that he should be compensated for his efforts. She gives him two thousand rupees, but is distraught that she has had to pay a bribe for getting a report lodged, which is her legal right as a citizen. Think about the following questions:

Do you think the cop was right in asking for a bribe to lodge a complaint?

Do you think Nimmi made the right choice in paying him two thousand rupees to lodge the complaint? Why?

What other alternatives could Nimmi choose?

Is the system also to blame here? Who constitutes the system?

A Bribe for a Wrong

Nimmi is riding her scooter to college early in the morning. She is late for her exam, and there is very little traffic. Seeing no traffic police around, she increases her speed to exceed the maximum limit. At the next corner, a traffic policeman suddenly steps out and signals for her to stop. Nimmi is taken aback. He tells her that she was over-speeding and asks for her license. Nimmi gets very nervous as she knows that she will be fined. She tries to argue that he is mistaken, and she was not over-speeding, but the cop refuses to yield. She tries to plead and request that he should let her go and promises not to repeat her mistake. The cop still does not relent. Nimmi then offers him five hundred rupees to allow her to leave. The cop quietly pockets the money and walks away. Nimmi is relieved and continues her journey to the college.

Think about the following questions:

> **Was Nimmi justified in over-speeding in the given situation?**
>
> **Do you think the cop should have let Nimmi off with a warning as it was a small violation and there was not much traffic?**
>
> **Was Nimmi justified in bribing the cop?**
>
> **Was the cop justified in accepting the bribe because she offered it without him asking for it?**

Nimmi is upset when the cop in the police station asks for a bribe to register a case for her lost mobile. But she gives it anyhow because her mobile cost twenty-five thousand and giving two thousand to find it was not much. When Nimmi is caught for over-speeding, she willingly offers a bribe to the traffic policeman to reach college in time for her exam and avoid paying a fine. Now ponder on these questions:

> **Do you see any contradictions in her behavior?**
>
> **Do you think the cops alone are to blame for dishonesty?**

How many instances of dishonesty do you find in these two situations?

Do you think it is acceptable to lie or pay a bribe when one is in a bad situation?

Do you think any damage was done to anyone by giving/taking bribes in these two situations?

Helping a Friend Cheat

Virendra is weak in Chemistry but cannot afford tuitions. He asks his friend Ashok to help him in the exam. Ashok passes him answers written on a slip. They manage not to be caught. Virendra passes in Chemistry and is promoted to the next class. He is very thankful to Ashok for helping him. Ashok, too, is happy that he has helped his friend. Think:

Considering his economic condition, was Virendra correct in cheating to avoid failing and repeating a year in the same class?

Was Ashok correct in helping him cheat? Did he do something good for his friend by helping him cheat? How?

Did it harm anyone if Virendra cheated to pass in chemistry? In what way?

When Merit doesn't Win

After Virendra finishes school, he applies for a scholarship in a professional college. There are only four seats, and the competition is fierce. But he is hopeful of getting the scholarship because he has enough marks and has given a good interview. He is disappointed to know that he has been rejected. A VIP's son, who had fewer marks than him, was adjusted by bending the rules. Virendra curses the system for being unfair and corrupt and ruining his future. Consider:

Was it fair for the college to adjust a VIP's son, when another student deserved the seat on merit?

Presuming that you are the Head of the professional college, can you defend your action?

Presuming that you are the VIP, can you defend your action?

Was Virendra justified in cursing the system that deprived him of the seat he felt he deserved? Why?

Now ponder this:

Do you see any contradictions in Virendra's behavior?

Does he have a right to feel upset with the system?

Who makes the system?

What are the results of a corrupt system?

Who has the power to change the system?

Do you think it affects only the individuals involved directly or has more far-reaching effects?

Arguments in Favor of Honesty

You might have come across many more real-life situations but never stopped to consider how dishonesty and deception are deeply infectious. The same person is sometimes at the giving end and sometimes at the receiving end. If we think that we can get away with lying and cheating to avoid an awkward situation, so will the others whom we interact with. We forgive our own dishonesty toward others but complain when we are at the receiving end of someone else's dishonesty. The only way there can be fair play in society is if the same rules for honesty apply to everyone.

In the first two situations, Nimmi complained when the cop at the police station asked for a bribe to register a complaint about her lost mobile but was quite happy to offer it when she violated the traffic rules by over-speeding. The cop was dishonest in demanding a bribe for doing his duty. Nimmi was dishonest by paying a bribe to lodge a complaint and lying about her speed and paying a bribe to avoid a challan. She was also responsible for encouraging dishonesty in the police force by offering bribes.

In the last two situations, Virendra went ahead and cheated to pass his chemistry exam. His friend Ashok felt that he had done a good deed by helping his friend. The ultimate aim of education is not passing an exam but learning the subject and enhancing our abilities so that we can apply them practically at a later stage. Virendra did not bother to work hard to learn chemistry, but depended on passing through cheating. Ashok did not do him a favor but contributed to making the system corrupt by helping him cheat. Neither was Ashok a sincere friend, as he did not advise him to choose the better option by offering to teach him to be better equipped for life. Virendra felt very disappointed when the college gave the scholarship to a VIP's son by bypassing him though he had more marks. It was another form of cheating. Virendra felt it was okay for him to cheat, but was upset when he himself became the victim.

The above examples make it quite clear how dishonesty has a way of spreading in society. If we do not want to become victims of deceit, let us enforce the same rules on ourselves. People frequently complain about the high levels of corruption in many government departments, politics, institutions, and job recruitment but surreptitiously promote it for their own benefit. It has led to a deterioration in standards of every service like governance, execution of public projects like building of roads, hospitals, bridges, and dams; core areas like education, medical facilities, and legal services.

Corruption in high places has also resulted in an ever-widening gap between the rich and the poor, denying basic needs to many people and hindering overall development and progress. Unfortunately, India ranks high in the list of corrupt countries, reflecting our country in a very poor light. Indians find it harder to get visitors visas to more developed countries and are looked at with suspicion and distrust by foreign consulates.

Advanced countries do not value Indian professional degrees and are not keen to hire Indian citizens for jobs. Most western countries do not recognize the medical and engineering degrees given by Indian universities and migrants must repeat courses to be eligible for employment. It speaks poorly of integrity in our educational standards.

Honesty affects a person's mental health, overall wellbeing, and relationships in many ways:

> **Honesty takes away fear from the heart and gives you courage. It is only the courageous who can stand up and speak the truth. Liars are cowards. They cannot face the truth and will keep on lying to back up one lie.**
>
> **People who lie always live under the stress of being exposed to others. They are continually looking over their shoulders. Their anxiety levels tend to be high, which makes them vulnerable to various diseases. People who choose to be truthful are at peace with themselves and**

the world. A person may buy some time through lying, but it will eventually catch up with him.

Dishonest people lose respect for themselves and suffer from low self-esteem and low self-confidence. Their dishonesty and lies are exposed to others at some time, and they lose respect in society. It may also cost them their job, invite penalty, or legal action.

Dishonesty spoils one's relationships with friends and family as people do not trust a dishonest person.

Cheating in exams may help you scrape through but will not qualify you for meeting challenges in your field. You are likely to fail in the interview or be thrown out for underperformance.

Shortcuts in life may appear to deliver immediate benefits but will eventually be detrimental.

Things to Ponder

Consider a situation when your old parent needs heart surgery. Would you like to take her to a doctor who has passed his exams by cheating? Could the doctor's medical knowledge make the difference between life and death for her?

Why do you think the politicians go abroad for their treatment?

If a bridge collapses while you drive over it, and leaves you severely injured, who will you hold responsible? The engineer who did not know his job because he cleared his exams by cheating, the teacher who allowed him to cheat, or a corrupt contractor who used substandard material in construction and pocketed part of the funds, or a corrupt official who accepted a bribe and cleared the bridge for safety standards?

A pharmaceutical company makes spurious drugs and sells them at high prices. The inspectors who are responsible for checking them for quality control accept bribes and take no action against them. Many people buy the spurious drugs and develop severe health conditions. Some lose their lives. Maybe the company owner is Virendra, the boy who felt it was okay to cheat in class 8? He probably went on to cheat in more significant ways until it became a way of life.

Do you think a student who resorts to cheating in his/her schooldays would continue doing so throughout life? Why/why not?

A politician gets election funds from big corporate houses. She wins the elections by bribing poor people for votes. There is no free lunch in this world. In return for the funds, she promises to favor the corporate houses who have funded her once she is in power. So the government policies she makes are not made for public welfare but for increasing benefits for the helpful corporates. Contracts for big business deals are also given to these companies instead of the more deserving ones. The politician takes her cut (maybe she used her influence to get the contract for building the bridge). Can you guess who this politician is? She is Nimmi, the girl who bribed the cops when she was a college student. As she grew up, she learned to use money in dishonest ways to achieve her own ends. A vicious circle of corruption comes into effect, causing multi-dimensional damage to ordinary citizens.

If you were a judge and the above cases were put up to you, would you hold them guilty? You most probably would. If yes, you would have understood the importance of honesty in everyday life, beginning from the small issues in childhood and leading to more significant ones later.

A Real-life Example

Kavaratti islands are a cluster of islands near the south-west tip of India. They are unique not only for their natural beauty but also for their people. The inhabitants of Kavaratti are not very rich, beautiful, or smart. Yet the island is unique for its culture. The inhabitants of this island are remarkably honest people who make a simple living through fishing and growing coconut trees. The one small jail on the island has never had an inmate! No one even touches a coconut that has fallen from a neighbor's tree. If you happen to drop your wallet on the road, you can be sure to find it when you go back to look for it. People live peacefully, and there are hardly any incidents of fights or domestic violence. They live happy and content lives, and hardly anyone is keen to leave the island for greener pastures.

3

Justice is not Blind

> Justice consists not in being neutral between right and wrong, but in finding out the right and upholding it, wherever found, against the wrong.
> —Theodore Roosevelt

Justice dictates that each person receives what he deserves. Depriving people of their rights and what is rightfully theirs amounts to injustice. Every civilized society functions within a system of law and punishment that applies to all its members. The system of justice protects people from exploitation, violence and other forms of crime. It gives them equal opportunity for progress and personal growth, expecting them to live together peacefully. No civilized societies can exist in the absence of laws or tools of justice. If a society descends into lawlessness, there is chaos leading to exploitation of the weaker sections, loss of life and property, and break down of the social order.

Justice is relevant not only at the political or larger social levels; it must be from childhood itself when children make small and seemingly unimportant choices. All of us want to be treated fairly. Injustice is hurtful and difficult to accept, often causing people to protest, rebel, or develop hostility against the propagator of injustice. As you will come to see, the virtue of justice is closely related to honesty. One cannot be learned or imbibed without the other.

Starting with the family unit, children expect that their parents treat all children equally. You would be upset if your sister received more pocket money than you, accusing your parents of being unjust. Students expect their teachers to treat all of them equally in class and not favor any one student over the other. They are right in doing so. Teachers should not treat some students better than others, as it would be unfair and unjust. Do you agree that rules to uphold justice apply to you too?

Social justice is commonly known as a movement toward equality of resources and rights. Many movements work to improve conditions of vulnerable or needy sections like destitute women and children, oppressed minorities, abandoned seniors, and so on. These movements spring from observing an injustice and searching for an implementable solution to it. Once a year, on World Day of Social Justice, we celebrate social justice movements worldwide and their impact.

Indian culture is an old and diverse culture credited with many noble traditions and contributions to humankind. Yet, it has also supported some of the most unjust and cruel social practices in which many groups of people are discriminated against based on community, religion, caste, and gender. As part of a larger society, many of us have unthinkably and unquestionably continued to carry on with these unjust social traditions even in this modern era. Despite stringent laws against discrimination, many people refuse to change their mindsets, perpetuating social prejudices and injustice through their attitudes and behavior.

The ultimate example of racial discrimination that existed in many countries was slavery, forcing people into servitude in homes, factories, and farms, and keeping them in deplorable conditions. You might think that slavery is a non-issue in the current world. However, it is still practiced around the world, albeit in hidden forms. About 40 million people worldwide are still trapped in some form of slavery, including marriage slavery and forced labor.

Segregation of people based on color and race has been a significant social justice issue. One historical example was the segregation of Black Americans in the U.S., where they were required to use separate schools, houses, medical services, institutions and facilities that were inferior to white Americans. Former U.S. President Obama's wife Michelle Obama gives an intimate account of an African American's life in her book *Becoming*. Another shameful example of segregation was apartheid in South Africa, where the Africans were segregated by the white races, and of ordinary Indians in British India. Many civil rights movements across the world challenged the unequal treatment and segregation of a cultural or racial group.

Recently, a lot of attention has been focused on discrimination based on sexuality and gender. In many places, women are still being paid less than men for similar work. Patriarchal social systems continue to deny women freedom of choice in choosing their life-partners and jobs, equality in education, right to work, and property inheritance.

Individuals of the Lesbian, Gay, Bisexual, Transsexual, and Queer (LGBTQ) community face several forms of social injustice and oppression. Transgender people often face discrimination, ridicule, and sexual exploitation in society.

Many people are still devoid of essential resources like potable water, nutritious food, housing, education, and health facilities. A large number of children are victims of sexual abuse and child labor.

Segregation in School

There are forty children in class VIII of the Government Senior Secondary School, Haripur. Ten of these students are from the backward classes. Their parents work as laborers in fields owned by families of the well-to-do students and as *safai sewaks* with the municipality. They wear worn-out and not-too-clean uniforms, with dirty shoes and shabby bags. Students complain that they smell bad. These ten students mostly sit together on the last bench in the class. They are aware that other

Is he really as different as you think?

children do not like to sit with them or play with them. In recess, they are made to sit in a separate line for receiving the mid-day meal.

Manjit is one of the disadvantaged students. She is a bright and hard-working girl who is particular about doing her homework and learning her lessons. However, her teacher is puzzled that she does not respond to questions in class even though she knows the answers. Her uniform is two years old and shabby. Her family cannot afford to buy a new one for her, and neither do they have the means to wash and iron it daily. She lives in a small house with a bathroom shared with three other families. On many days, Manjit does not get an opportunity to take a bath before coming to school because the bathroom is occupied. So, she tends to smell in summer. All these factors lower her self-esteem and prevent her from responding in class, even though she knows the answer. Her friend Sundari is an outstanding singer but is never included in any function by the teacher because she does not have a presentable uniform to wear on the stage.

What do you think:

Are all people born equal? Can you tell the caste or religion of a newborn baby?

Are students from backward classes capable of doing as well as others in the class?

Is it possible for society to function without the so-called low-level services rendered by their parents?

Is it fair that Manjit's performance is affected because of her adverse circumstances? Who is responsible for it?

What could you do to help Manjit and Sundari?

Racism at Home

Farida is a class IX student in the Government School of Nurpur. Her family has migrated from Andhra Pradesh, and she is the only Muslim girl in the class. Farida cannot speak Punjabi. She wears a head-scarf and carries south-Indian food in her tiffin, which smells different from Punjabi food. Her classmates treat her as an outsider. They often make fun of her scarf, language, and food. One day she brought some sweets made by her mother and offered them to Kamla, who sits next to her. Kamla refused to accept the sweets saying that she could not have food made in a Muslim household. Farida was very upset and started crying. She told her father that she did not want to continue with her schooling.

Think about this:

People from different cultures, states, and religions speak different languages and have different dress styles and food habits. Can you say that it makes them any better or worse than the other?

Does food become unclean if cooked by people of a different faith? Are you aware of who prepares your McDonald burgers, medicines, or pizzas?

Racism Abroad

Suhail Singh has moved to New Zealand with his family and joined a school there. He finds it very difficult to adjust because he does not comprehend English well and cannot follow the teacher's lectures or classmates' accents. Some students make fun of his turban. They also find it very odd that he is a vegetarian while they are non-vegetarians. His classmates think he has come from some backward country and treat him as an outsider. Suhail loses self-confidence and does poorly in class even though he was a good student in India. He tells his parents that he does not want to go to school. His mother is distraught at the treatment meted out to him and complains of discrimination to the school principal.

Think about the following questions:

What are the reasons for the white students' racist behavior towards Suhail?

Imagine yourself in Suhail's place. What would you do?

What can be the possible results of racism?

Do you find it difficult to accept people who are different? Why?

Is racism of any kind acceptable? Why?

Ponder over these points:

Many of you aspire to go to Canada, Australia, or New Zealand for higher studies or work. How will you feel if the people of that country treat you as a lesser human and look down upon you? Will you protest or accept it without complaining?

Is it unjust to deny equality to all, or are some people superior to others?

History tells us that Indians were not allowed to enter British clubs or first-class railway compartments when India was a British colony. How does that make you feel?

Is it correct to treat people of your country, or those of any other nationality or race, in the same hateful way, regarding them as inferior? What would you say to a person who does this?

Does skin color or shape of their eyes and nose make people inferior or superior? Does it affect people's attitudes? Why?

Prejudices born out of ignorance

Denying fundamental equality and respect to any person based on his or her caste, creed, race, religion, or nationality is not only unjust but a crime against humanity. India is a secular country. Its constitution gives all citizens equal rights regardless of their religion, race, caste, or creed. If someone insults or hurts a person or group from the minorities, he/she can be prosecuted under law. No one is better or worse than the other because of their skin color, features, religion, language, dress or food habits. People from the North-east or the South look very different from North-Indians. Does that make them lesser persons in any way?

Tenzing Norgay, an Indian of Nepali origin, was one of the first two individuals to reach Mount Everest's summit in 1953. Times nominated him as one of the 100 most influential people of the 20th century.

South-Indians have their own dress style, language, and culture. They are often collectively and foolishly referred to as 'Madrassis' by North-Indians, though they come from various states. Look at these examples below of South-Indians who brought laurels to the country.

The first Indian, Asian, and non-white scientist to be awarded the Nobel Prize in 1930, Dr. CV Raman belonged to Tamil Nadu. Subrahmanyam Chandrashekhar, a physicist from Tamil Nadu, was also awarded the Nobel Prize in 1983.

Homi Jehangir Bhabha was a famous atomic scientist responsible for creating two premier research institutes of India—the Tata Institute of Fundamental Research and the Bhabha Atomic Research Centre. He belonged to the minority community of Parsis.

APJ Abdul Kalam, the 11th President of India, was an aerospace scientist. He was a Muslim from Tamil Nadu, and came to be known as the Missile Man of India for his work on the development of ballistic missiles, strengthening our country's security and defense.

All these outstanding persons belonged to communities and religions you may not be very familiar with as students born and raised in Punjab. It is common for people to regard unfamiliar and different others with suspicion and hostility. But they might be much better people than you are. The foundation of Harmandir Sahib, regarded as the holiest shrine of the Sikhs, was laid by a Muslim Sufi saint, Hazrat Mian Mir. By giving him this honor, Guru Arjan Dev again underlined Guru Nanak Dev's messages, which said,

"Manas ki zaat sabe eko pehchanbo."
(Treat the entire human race as one.)

"Na ko Hindu na Mussalman."
(There are no Hindus or Muslims, meaning they are all the same)

"Awall Allah noor upaya, kudrat ke sab bande.
Ek noor te sab jag upjaya, kaun bhale ko mande."

**(All humanity has risen from the divine light created by God.
The entire world has risen from this divine light, and there are no good or bad people.)**

The Sikh gurus and social reformers like BR Ambedkar, Rabindranath Tagore, Mahatma Gandhi, Jyotiba Phule, and Begum Rokeya fought for social justice in Indian society. It is an ongoing struggle which each of us must take forward.

4

Respect

The right to be respected is won by respecting others.
—Vasyl Sohkomlynsky

Respect is the sense of worth or personal value that someone holds in your eyes. Respect cannot be demanded; it must be earned through virtue of the goodness of your thoughts and actions, from how well you treat others, how just, truthful, compassionate and respectful you are to others. Respect comes to you when you are a productive, law-abiding, loyal, dutiful and dependable person. Understandably, some people earn more respect than others through their personal merits. Still, the bottom line to live by is that all human beings, animals and nature deserve our respect.

What is respect? Is it something that comes out of fear? Is it something that you feel for someone more powerful than you? Is it something that you show someone to get some benefit? Should respect be associated with factors like people's station in life, wealth, caste, skin color, or gender? Is respect due only to people placed above you, are stronger or older? They say that if you want to judge how evolved a culture is, see how they treat their old people, women, and those who serve them.

Additionally, a person can be judged by how he treats the physically disabled, mentally challenged, those different in other ways, and weaker or lower in status. Respect is closely connected to being just and without prejudice, to being kind and sensitive to others. We also need to know what disrespectful behavior is to identify it and refrain from it. It includes:

Showing disregard for people's rights, feelings, and convenience. In short, being selfish.

Breaking the law, ignoring social norms, or creating a disturbance.

Lying, stealing, or cheating.

Disruptive behavior such as angry or rude outbursts, verbal threats, swearing and bullying.

Exploiting someone's weakness or vulnerabilities with demeaning comments, fault-finding, insults or insensitive jokes and sarcasm.,

Intimidating someone through threats, abuse of power, or force of personality. It includes dominating and arrogant behavior, and intentionally forcing oneself into another person's personal space.,

To begin with, respect for others will come if you respect yourself. Self-respect is earned through imbibing qualities capable of respect. You cannot respect yourself if you lie, cheat, steal, or abuse others, and neither will others respect you. Moreover, if you keep low benchmarks of behaviour for yourself, you will expect the same from others and live in an ugly world of suspicion and hostility. When you look at the mirror and see someone you can respect, you can be sure others will respect you.

It might be hard to believe, but it is most challenging to earn respect in one's own eyes. One may lie or pretend to the world, but one can neither lie nor pretend to oneself. Every time you do something that goes against your conscience's voice, you lose respect in your own eyes. You might clear an exam through cheating or make a lot of money by fooling someone, but you will end up feeling smaller instead of happier.

If you give in to your friends' unfair demands due to peer pressure, realizing that they are not in your best interests, you lose self-respect and respect in their eyes.

You lose self-respect when you compromise your values for some personal gain, when you are mean or unfair to someone else.

Respect for the Feelings of Others

We sometimes see people behaving in cruel ways around us. How often have you come across incidences when you want to advise people to:

Not make fun of people, mock or tease them.

Show respect for people with disabilities; people who are less smart than them and caught up in an unfavorable situation.

Not look down upon people who are placed lower in social status, and be polite while interacting with household helpers, laborers, rickshaw pullers, children, waiters and peons.

Use 'please' and 'thank you' while interacting with others.

Listen attentively when someone speaks, instead of taking phone calls or checking messages on the mobile.

Not talk ill of people behind their backs. Gossip eventually tends to reach back to the person. It hurts the person's feelings and shows you up as a malicious person.

Respect for Equal Rights of Others

Know your rights to understand how you should be treated and how you should treat others. Understand equality-human beings are born free and equal and have the same rights as anyone else.

No one should use another human being for personal advantage but respect his/her rights as an individual.

No person should be discriminated against based on country, race, creed, language, religion, political opinion or social status.

No one should be put through fear, oppression, torture or any other cruelty or punishment that makes one feel less than human.

All human beings should be treated equally by the law.

Everyone, including women, LGBTQ, the disabled, and challenged, has an equal right to education.

All human beings have freedom of opinion and information and the right to express their views without fear.

Respect for Personal Differences

Respect people who are different from you. Remember that the world we live in is hugely diverse. People from other countries, cultures, races, and religions are all worthy of equal respect. Do not think that your country, race, culture, or religion is the best? People who have different skin color, features, speak a foreign language, dress differently, or have other eating habits or sexual inclinations are all equally good and maybe better than us in certain respects. Your nation, culture, or group is not the center of the world. Even our world is but a speck in the universe.

Respect different opinions and choices which people have. Everyone does not and need not think alike. One may discuss different viewpoints and ideologies, but do it with an open mind and with due respect to others. It should not involve insults, personal attacks or fights. People must be allowed to make their choices and hold their opinions.

Do not stereotype people based on false inputs. Calling a specific community dirty, labeling a race stupid because they are materially backward, calling a whole nation dishonest because of propaganda is disrespectful, discriminatory and false.

Respect for Family

Respect your parents, grandparents, and extended family members. Many youngsters feel that their parents are too controlling. Nevertheless, they have greater experience in the world and are much more qualified to make decisions in a teenager's interest. A teenager's brain is yet not fully developed and functional, leading them to take immature and impulsive decisions, which can be damaging. Do not treat your parents merely as someone to provide facilities and care for you. They deserve love, respect, and appreciation for working hard and sacrificing their own needs to fulfil your requirements. Parents are ordinary men and women who may have some shortcomings. They are not perfect; no one is. They deserve to be respected nevertheless.

Extend help and love to your grandparents. Survival depends on cooperation. Will you expect your children and grandchildren to help you when you are their age?

Respect for Women

Starting with your family, respect your mother and sisters. Do not think that boys have more rights than girls; the same diet, facilities and freedom should be available to both boys and girls.

Household duties should be shared among male and female family members. Boys can wash and iron their clothes, and cook just as well, and should not expect their mothers and sisters to do these chores for them.

Controlling girls and women through threats or violence is unjust and disrespectful. They have a right to freedom, study time and leisure, socializing and sports as much as boys.

Why don't boys?

Give due respect to your mother and honor her contribution to the family. Do not treat her as someone who exists to cook and take care of others.

Treating girls as objects of amusement or fun is disrespectful. Teasing, making rude or obscene remarks, harassing girls, sending offensive messages, making persistent phone calls, and clicking pictures without consent is disrespectful, rude and punishable.

Sharing nude pictures or pornographic material on your phone or posting them on social media is unacceptable and punishable.

Respect for Rules

Whether it is small or large, members of a group must respect the group's rules for it to function well. A family is a primary group with the parents as rule-makers. Follow the rules set by your parents. If your parents tell you to be home before dark, set study hours for you and give you specific duties, you must go by the given rules.

Larger groups outside the home include schools, colleges, offices, and other religious and social groups. Every member must follow the rules of these groups for optimum performance and peaceful co-existence.

You are also a member of larger groups like the city, state, and nation. Rules set by them take the form of law. Every citizen must follow the law for maintaining peace and order.

Follow the traffic rules. Do not drive a vehicle before you are eighteen. Carry your driving license at all times. If you happen to hit someone, stop and help the person and take him/her to the hospital if needed. Hit and run is an offense. Jumping red lights or driving motorbikes without a silencer is punishable under the law. Playing loud music in the car creates a public nuisance.

There are many who do not respect public property and deface historical monuments, walls, toilets and public vehicles by scratching or writing on them. How do you feel if you board a bus and are allotted a seat which has a torn cover and scratched paint? Are you repulsed by graffiti on the walls of a public toilet? Damaging public property in any way is a crime against society.

You will see many people who don't follow the rules and seem to prosper despite it. We can change ourselves, but we cannot change the world. So, how should we deal with the situation to survive?

You cannot force someone to respect you, but you can refuse to be disrespected or mistreated.

Shun disrespectful people and bullies who show no regard for people, laws, morality, or social norm. Do not tolerate people who explain their rude or inconsiderate behavior by saying, 'That's just how I am.'

Do not retaliate with disrespect and insult to hold your ground.

Remember that rudeness is the weak person's imitation of strength.

Never respond to rudeness. When people are rude to

you, they reveal who they are, not who you are. Don't take it personally, be silent, and walk away.

Fun at the Teacher's Expense

Sunil is not interested in studies. He failed in class last year and is repeating his term in class X. As a result, he is older than other students and tries to boss over them. When the teacher was writing on the blackboard during the Math class, Sunil started mimicking him behind his back, making the students laugh. The teacher turned around and enquired about the reason for laughter. No one spoke up because they were afraid of Sunil. When this was repeated, the teacher refused to teach further until he was told who was disturbing the class. Pankaj gathered courage and told the teacher that Sunil was the mischief-maker. The teacher turned Sunil out of the class. Sunil confronted Pankaj after school and threatened to teach him a lesson for telling on him.

Is respect important?

Questions to think about:

What is Sunil trying to achieve by raising laughter at the expense of the teacher? Concerning the incident, what do you think could be the different thoughts and reactions of the students?

Can you gain knowledge from your teachers without respect for them?

Is it correct for Sunil to threaten Pankaj? What can be the results of disrespect for one's classmates?

Do you think Sunil is unsuccessful due to his attitude? What kind of a man do you see Sunil in the future? To what extent do you believe Sunil's present attitude will contribute to shaping him into the man he will become?

What should be your attitude towards your teachers and authorities in society: ridicule or respect? Why?

Lack of Tolerance

Tina has organized a party for her fifteenth birthday. She has invited many friends for the party and laid out a grand feast for them. All are dancing to the music and enjoying themselves. Their household helper, Rekha, while carrying the birthday cake to the table, collides with a guest, loses her balance, and drops it. Tina flies into a rage and abuses her in front of everyone. Rekha is distraught and tells her that Tina has insulted her in front of everyone because she is poor. If her sister had dropped the cake, would she have abused her the same way? Tina fires Rekha for being clumsy and insolent.

Questions to think about:

Was it correct for Tina to insult Rekha in front of all the guests?

Was it justified for Rekha to answer back?

Do you think what Rekha said was correct? Do people feel they have the right to insult poor people?

Do you think that poor people have no right to respect?

Have you noticed that most people tend to address rickshaw pullers, safai sewaks, and domestic workers as 'tu' instead of 'tussi' or 'aap'? Is it justified?

As a worker, will you prefer an employer who pays you very well but does not respect you or an employer who pays you less but gives you respect? Why?

Respecting Women

Dinkar is the only son of his parents, with two elder sisters. His parents have always given him special treatment, so he has come to believe that he has a special status and rights in the family. He expects his mother to serve him food, and his sisters to wash and iron his clothes and clean his room. Dinkar spends his time playing and relaxing without contributing to any work in the house. In contrast, his mother and sisters work hard. One day he scolds his elder sister for standing out in the street and talking to her classmate, saying that it was not the right thing to do for girls.

Questions to think about:

Is Dinkar respectful towards his mother and sisters by expecting them to do his work?

Do you think that cooking, washing clothes, and cleaning the house are women's work alone? Why?

Do people respect women's rights if they assign all household work to them?

Do you agree that speaking to her classmate in the street will make his sister lose respect? Or is it Dinkar who disrespects his sister?

Do you have a similar scenario in your home? What efforts will you make to change such a set up there?

Respect for Individual Choices

Neera and Manish are friends, and they often spend time together. Neera likes to go out with him to shop, see movies, and have ice cream. One day Manish invited her to come home. When she went to his house, she found that his parents had gone out. Manish tried to make physical contact with her. Neera refused. Manish wanted to force himself on her, saying that girls do not mean it when they refuse. Neera was very upset at his behavior and broke off her relationship with him. Manish says he loves her very much and cannot stay without her. He blackmails her, threatening to circulate her intimate pictures on social media. Manish says that she has no right to reject him after having a relationship with him. Neera is scared that he will tarnish her reputation and agrees to continue the relationship with him.

Questions to think about:

Did Manish show respect for Neera when he tried to force himself on her despite her refusal?

Do boys have a right to expect physical intimacy if they are friends with a girl?

Was Manish respectful when he blackmailed Neera? Do you think he really loved her?

Was Neera's decision to continue meeting him correct? What were the risks she was taking by her decision?

Did Neera show any respect for herself by giving in to Manish's blackmail? How would you have acted had you been in Manish/Neera's place?

Respect for Differences

Seerat and Keerat are both students of class X. They both belong to different religions, say A and B. Both girls profess to be deeply religious. Whenever Seerat talks about religion A, Keerat immediately starts to talk about how religion B is better than A. Seerat contradicts her by giving examples. Eventually, both end up fighting bitterly. Other students in the class also start taking sides depending on whether they belong to religion A or B. Soon, the class is divided into two warring groups.

Questions to think about

Do people who follow different religions pray to different gods?

If someone disrespects another religion, do you think she is disrespecting God?

Is it possible for everyone in the world to have the same faith?

Are some religions better than others?

Do you think the formation of two warring groups in the class is likely to be repeated on a larger scale in society if we disrespect other religions?

Introspection

Nancy has gone to the market. Unable to find a parking slot for her scooter, she parks it behind a car, and proceeds for shopping. She returns after half-an-hour to find an old gentleman waiting to take his car out. Nancy apologizes to him and removes her scooter. When Nancy parked her scooter behind the car, she knew that the owner would not be able to remove his car. Yet she ignored his inconvenience. Her apology to him later was not sincere and merely a cover-up.

You want to go out for a picnic with your friends, but your parents refuse permission. You lie to them that you are going to a friend's house to study. You are not only showing disrespect to your parents by lying to them and betraying their trust, but you are also disrespecting yourself by lying.

Ben wants to be part of a group of students in his class. They insist that he try out some drugs at a party. He does not want to but is so keen on being accepted as one of them that he agrees to try the drugs. Ben has shown a lack of self-respect and self-confidence by giving in to his peer group's unfair and dangerous demand. The peer group has also shown disrespect towards Ben by forcing him to do something he does not want.

A new teacher comes to the class. She is not dressed well. Nina's friends make fun of her, but Nina does not join them. They think Nina is trying to win her favor and make fun of her too. Nina's friends are disrespectful towards the teacher and Nina both. Nina has shown self-respect by not following the group and respect for the teacher.

Historical Examples of Disrespect for Human Dignity

Slavery existed in many cultures starting from early civilizations. Slavery means treating human beings as disposable property, without rights or privileges.

Colonization occurs when a country takes control of other lands or regions outside its borders by turning them into a colony. It is done for economic gains or in search of a better life. Europeans established their colonies in America, Africa, Asia (including India). In such a state, the colonized countries are treated as servants or slaves to produce wealth and comfort for the colonizers.

Racism still exists in the U.S. today, but it is debatable how pervasive and influential it is. Many people point to high poverty rates and unemployment among blacks as strong evidence that racism is still very powerful.

The lack of respect shown to Indians by the British gave an impetus to the freedom movement. Similarly, the dehumanization of the slaves in America led to the Civil War and the abolition of slavery through the Slavery Abolition Act.

India's caste system has been the most persistent social problem. Members of the low caste are looked down upon by members of high castes. People from lower castes have been denied human dignity, elementary civil, and political rights and treated unjustly for centuries. Several laws have now been put in place to fight this disrespect shown to the lower caste people.

Summing Up

People can co-exist in peace and harmony only if they show mutual respect for each other's rights, opinions, property, and wishes.

Respect must be shown to all: women, people from lower social status, elders, younger people, strangers, people belonging to different races and cultures.

Stereotyping leads to discrimination against specific communities and women, robbing them of fundamental rights like freedom, equality, fraternity, dignity, and opportunities to grow.

You can expect people to show respect to you only if you show them respect.

Respect must be shown for thought and opinion, which may be different from yours. You must be able to argue with respect.

Giving respect to your family members, teachers, friends, and all those you interact with generates cooperation and goodwill, making the world a better place.

5

Compassion and Empathy

> Love and compassion are necessities, not luxuries. Without them, humanity cannot survive.
> —Dalai Lama

Imagine your car develops a snag on a lonely road in a strange town, and you are standing by the roadside. What will you hope for? Perhaps for a compassionate traveler to stop and help you. You would probably do the same if you came across a stranded traveler in your city. Compassion involves empathy for others and the desire to help them. Empathy is the ability to connect with people to understand their feelings and behavior. It is to put ourselves in another person's place and imagine how we would feel in a similar situation. It makes us aware of a person's suffering and motivates us to help. Compassionate behavior nurtures humanity by helping the receiver and bringing happiness and joy to the giver.

Look at it like this. The society you live in is like a human bank. You will, someday, surely get back what you deposit in it today. If you help a classmate today, she will most likely help you out when you need help. If you run down a person, he will look for an opportunity to hit you back. With this logic, if you help a stranger on the road, it is likely that she will also be motivated to help someone at another time and place. Positivity and negativity both tend to spread. It is for us to choose and shape the kind of world we want to live in. There is a saying: 'What goes around, comes around'.

Sometimes you may feel confused because justice and compassion seem to be at odds with each other. If your friend has wronged you, you may think that justice demands that you react to punish him. But compassion demands that you forgive him. In such situations, you are faced with a conflict between feelings of anger, hurt, revenge on one side, and a calling for compassion on the other side. Should you follow your emotions or your higher conscience? If you are caught in this kind of situation, put yourself in your friend's position and think. Would you like to be forgiven or punished? Every child makes mistakes some time or the other. Sometimes the parents punish the child, but many a time, they let him off with a warning. That is compassion. It would not be easy to exist if justice were to be preferred over compassion every time. Compassion is greater than justice, though both have to be used with much thought.

Empathy is the first step toward compassion. Sometimes we are outraged when people lie, cheat, or act in ways to damage or hurt others, and are justified in demanding due punishment for them. In our anger, we forget to look into their backgrounds and personality problems, which might have led them to make the wrong choice. If we want to make positive changes to the system, we will have to empathize to understand and rectify the causes behind the person's improper behavior. The reason behind a girl's rude and aggressive behavior might lie in harsh family circumstances. A boy who is into drug abuse may be escaping the difficult challenges of life, which he feels unable to cope with. According to a Native American proverb, 'Walk a mile in another man's shoes before you criticize him.'

A mistake most of us make is to prejudge people without knowing them. We already 'know' how girls think and behave, which communities are aggressive, which religions are intolerant and which nations are adverse to us. If you were to justify the reasons for your assessment, you would not be able to do so, except that 'this is what people say'. And the people who say so would likewise give the same reason, perpetuating many such myths. Such ignorant and misplaced preconceptions take away from empathizing with groups other than our own, narrowing down and prejudicing our perspectives.

Genuine, focused listening is the essential art of understanding people. Let us be open to know other people; to listen to them carefully, and understand their emotions and circumstances. It lays the base for communication, which is essential to empathy. Strip your minds of all the junk which society has piled up in them about 'other' religions, communities, and nations. Once you make an effort to get to know them personally, you will realize the falsehood of these claims. There is no 'other'; only us.

Courtesy involves polite and considerate behavior towards others. Being courteous means thinking of other people before yourself; it means being kind and caring towards people. Courtesy demands that we do not say anything or behave in a way that is insulting towards others or hurts their feelings. Courtesy, empathy, and compassion are interconnected. Extending common courtesies to your family, friends, classmates, teachers, and even strangers come from being an educated and cultured person with good human values. It has to be a way of life.

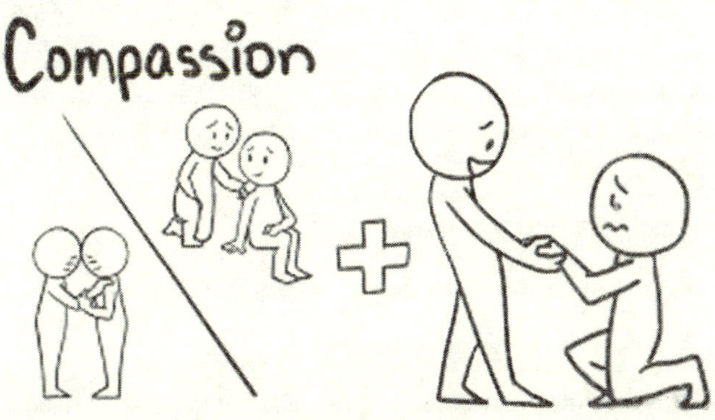

Compassion to the Hungry

During the coronavirus pandemic, many migrant laborers were without shelter or enough food. Neelam prepared food packets for them. Her father was angry that she was giving away precious rations. He was uncertain about the lifting of curfew and access to more rations.

Questions for you:

Do you think Neelam did the right thing?

Do you think her father's worry was correct?

Is it a collective responsibility of all to take care of each other during bad times?

Is sacrifice also a part of compassion sometimes?

Did you try putting yourself in place of the migrant laborers during the lockdown? What do you think could be done to help them?

Corona Scare

Health authorities have cordoned off a house in the neighborhood because it has a COVID-19 patient. There are four adults and two children in the family. Everyone in the area is terrified of going near that house. Milk and vegetable vendors have stopped giving them supplies.

Questions to think about:

How do you think the neighbors should help them?

What do the neighbors lack here?

Do you think this could happen to any family?

What will you expect if your family is in a similar condition?

Hunger and Theft

Naresh is a student of class 5. He is caught stealing food from his friend Rahul's tiffin during recess. Rahul is very annoyed with him and reports him to his teacher, saying that Naresh has done this more than once. What do you think his teacher should do? You can choose more than one option:

Find out the possible reasons why Naresh stole food.

Punish him by humiliating him in front of the whole class to set an example for other children.

Call him separately and ask him the reason for stealing, explaining why it is a wrong thing to do.

Call both the boys and ask Naresh to apologize to Rahul.

Call his parents and complain to them about him.

Sharing

Manjit and Shirin sit together in class. Shirin's mother is ill and cannot cook for her in the morning, so she comes to school without breakfast and does not carry any tiffin either. Manjit starts bringing more food in her tiffin so that she can share it with Shirin.

Questions to think about:

Does Manjit show empathy or charity in sharing her tiffin with her friend?

Will Manjit's gesture cement their friendship better?

Do you think that Manjit's gesture will inspire other students in their class?

Is it important that the benefit of compassion should come back to you?

Compassion for the Elderly

Jagan travels to his school by a local bus daily. The bus is generally crowded with students and office-going people, and many of them go standing. Jagan boards the bus first, so he can find a seat. Most days, he finds a woman or a senior citizen standing without a seat. He always gets up and offers his seat to such passengers and stands through the twenty-minute journey. His friends think it is stupid and laugh at him.

Questions to think about:

Should youngsters offer a seat to older people and women in trains, buses, and public places?

How will you feel if your grandmother had to stand through twenty minutes of travel by bus?

Are Jagan's friends more practical than him?

Equality

Thomas has two sisters, Amy and Daisy. He gets a glass of milk with breakfast every day, while his sisters get tea. Whenever his mother cooks chicken, she picks out the best pieces for Thomas and his father. They also get to eat a larger quantity than the girls. His parents say that boys and men need more nutrition than girls to grow strong. Thomas takes it for granted that males are entitled to better food.

Questions to think about:

Do you think the distribution of food in Thomas's home is fair?

Is it correct that boys need more food to grow strong? Is girls' health less important?

What is lacking in the men of this family?

Will you protest if this happens in your family?

Justice or Compassion

Nathu has been convicted for murder. He had a brawl with his friend Mahesh in a drunken state, killing him unknowingly. Mahesh's lawyer and family want him hanged. Nathu's lawyer begs mercy, saying that it happened in a fit of drunken rage and was not a deliberate crime.

Questions to think about:

Is Nathu innocent or guilty?

What is the demand for justice?

What is the demand for compassion?

What judgment would you pass if you were the judge?

Victory or Compassion

Kenyan runner Abel Mutai led the cross-country race at an event in Burlada, Navarre, in December 2012, when he mistakenly thought he'd crossed the finish line and pulled up. He was still about 32 feet before the actual finish line. Spanish runner Ivan Fernandez Anaya, who was running in the second place, had the opportunity to grab the gold, but he didn't. Instead of exploiting Mutai's mistake and claiming an unlikely victory, he stayed behind and, through gestures, guided his rival to the line to cross it first. When the journalist asked him why he allowed the Kenyan to win, he replied, "He was the rightful winner. If I had won, what would be the merit of my victory? What would be the honor of that medal? What would my Mom think of that? My dream is that someday we can have a kind of community life because today, with the way things are in all circles: in soccer, in society, in politics, where it seems anything goes, a gesture of honesty goes down well." Fernandez Anaya chose compassion and empathy over victory.

Questions to think about:

Why did Fernandez Anaya call Abel Mutai the rightful winner?

What quality did Fernandez Anaya exhibit through his behavior?

Do you believe that all is fair in love and war?

Did Fernandez win more respect through his exemplary behavior than if he had won the race?

Historical Example

Bhai Kanahiya was a disciple of Guru Gobind Singh. During frequent battles between the Sikhs and the Mughals, Bhai Kanhaiya was often seen carrying a *Mashak* (a large pouch made of goat's skin used to carry water) to serve water to anyone thirsty. He took upon the task of quenching the wounded soldiers' thirst in the battle of Anandpur Sahib in 1704. He carried out this service without any discrimination between the Sikh soldiers and the Mughal army soldiers. His act of compassion stirred up criticism amongst his fellow Sikhs. They were especially annoyed because the Mughals had surrounded the city and stopped all their food supplies, while Bhai Kanhaiya shared with them the little water they had. They tried to stop him, but he replied that he did not see the wounded soldiers as Sikhs or Muslims but only as suffering humans who deserved compassion. They complained about him to Guru Gobind Singh. The Guru appreciated Bhai Kanhayia for his compassion, saying that he had understood humanity in the real sense.

Summing Up

Compassion and empathy are interconnected. Humanity cannot exist without these virtues. Practicing compassion affects others to do likewise, and goodness spreads for the betterment of society. Empathy involves placing yourself in someone's position to understand what they are going through. The world would be a very harsh place to live in without these two virtues.

6

Courage

> Courage is the greatest of all virtues, because if you haven't courage, you may not have an opportunity to use any of the others.
> —Samuel Johnson

> I learned that courage was not the absence of fear but the triumph over it. The brave man is not he who does not feel afraid, but he who conquers that fear.
> —Nelson Mandela

When we talk of courage, the images that rush to our minds are of heroes like Guru Gobind Singh, Mahatma Gandhi, Swami Vivekanand, B.R. Ambedkar, Begum Hazrat Mahal, Nelson Mandela and Bhagat Singh. And indeed, they were all very courageous people. They stood up and fought against tyranny and exploitation of the weak even when the odds were heavily against them, making tremendous sacrifices in the process. But contrary to popular belief, courage is not superhuman. It co-exists with fear in most of us and can manifest itself in many ways. Courage does not necessarily mean wielding a gun to fight wars; it does not mean hunting down tigers or performing difficult physical feats. We are called upon to display courage in many small choices we make in our daily lives. What then is courage?

Courage is the personal ability to deal with challenging and tough circumstances, many a time at considerable risk to one's safety. It is the willingness to confront fear, pain, unknown danger and apprehensions. A large part of developing courage is having faith in yourself, which comes from cultivating a positive attitude. A courageous mindset is the product of faith and confidence in oneself and a positive outlook.

Showing courage includes:

Owning up our mistakes at the cost of being punished

Shunning the temptation of taking the unethical but easy way out of a dilemma.

Standing up and supporting what is right at the cost of personal risk. Brave people often take a moral stand and have a clear sense of purpose.

Supporting a weaker person without any personal stake.

Resisting peer pressure at the risk of being unpopular.

Opposing the majority to support the right cause at the risk of becoming an outcast. You need courage to express ideas that go against popular views, resulting in hostility or ridicule for departing from social norms.

Standing up against a stronger person or institution to condemn what is wrong, even though they hold power to damage us.

To put it simply, courage is not the absence of fear, but the ability to overcome fear, uncertainty, pain, pressure, threat and danger to make the choices you believe in. Courage is siding with the truth and protesting against tyranny, and all that is wrong. Defenders of human rights are some of the bravest people in the world today.

Ten Qualities of Courageous People

Courageous people have confidence in themselves and their choices.

They have a clear belief system that they are ready to defend at any cost.

They are driven by strong goals.

They can take risks to attain their goals.

They can resist pressure from friends and society to take a stand for what they believe.

They do not seek popularity at the cost of values.

They are ready to face danger in pursuance of their goals.

They own up to their weaknesses and mistakes without losing self-esteem.

They are capable of making sacrifices for the sake of their beliefs.

They have personal integrity.

They can go against the majority and are not afraid of facing criticism.

Courage to Help

Bina is traveling by a local train late in the evening. She sees a group of four rowdy boys teasing a girl who is traveling alone. There are only a few more passengers in the coupe. The girl tries to fend them off, but they persist in bothering her. She is frightened and almost in tears, but no one comes to her rescue as they are scared of the goons. Bina is furious but aware that she is not physically strong enough to tackle the boys alone. She imagines herself in the same situation and decides to take action. Bina appeals to the passengers to stop the boys from misbehaving and threatens to pull the chain. Though she is afraid that they will attack her when she gets off at the station, she decides to take the risk anyhow. The passengers follow her lead to stop the goons from harassing the girl.

Questions to think about:

If Bina were your sister, would you suggest her to take a similar stand and put herself at risk? Be honest.

If the girl who is being harassed were your sister, would you want Bina to take a similar risk to help her?

Do you think it was a social duty of the other passengers in the coupe to come to the girl's rescue?

Is it correct that we expect help when we are in trouble but are often unwilling to extend it to others?

Courage to Refuse

Shaheen is new in school and does not have any friends yet. She is happy when some of her classmates invite her to have lunch with them during recess. But Shaheen is uncomfortable when they ask her to bunk classes and join them for a movie. She knows that they will not accept her as a part of the group if she refuses, but not wanting to miss out on her lectures; she excuses herself from accompanying them.

Come on, join us.

Questions to think about:

Did Shaheen show courage by refusing to join the girls?

Which other personal quality did she show?

Do you think she will be able to make any friends in the class? Why?

Can you recall a situation where you had to choose against your friends?

Loyalty vs. Ethics

Manoj and his friends study in the hostel. They decide to have a late-night party in Tony's room to celebrate his birthday, and smuggle in some beer that is banned in the hostel. The next morning, the warden finds empty beer bottles in the garbage. During the morning assembly, he asks the culprit to step forward and confess. No one steps up. The warden announces that no one will be allowed out of the hostel till the culprits own up. Manoj feels guilty that others should suffer for what they had done, and requests his friends to own up. His friends refuse and say that he is crazy to suggest it. Manoj feels guilty and goes to the warden and admits that they had brought beer into the hostel. All the boys are punished. Manoj's friends are very angry with him for letting them down. They say he lost nerve and is a coward.

Questions to think about:

Do you think it is more important to be loyal to your friends or listen to your conscience?

Suppose you were one of the boys who did not attend the party but were shut up in the hostel due to what others did? What would you want them to do?

Do you think Manoj was a coward?

Do you think the other boys were brave in not owning up?

Courage to Refuse

Jaggi is a fifteen-year-old girl from village Maddi. She has just finished her tenth class and plans to go into professional sports in college. Her parents have six children and are keen to get Jaggi married off. Jaggi does not want to get married yet and wants to study further. Her parents refuse to listen to her wishes and go ahead and fix up her marriage. They beat her up when she resists. Jaggi discusses her problem with her friend Veera, who suggests that she approach her grandparents to talk to her parents. Jaggi's grandparents refuse to support her. Veera then suggests that she lodge a complaint with the police, and offers to accompany her to the police station.

Jaggi is initially scared of lodging a complaint against her parents but finally agrees. Both girls go to the police station and lodge a complaint against Jaggi's parents for forcing a minor into marriage. Jaggi is moved into a girl's home by the police and evades a forced marriage.

Questions to think about:

Should Jaggi have obeyed her parents, or was it right for her to take a stand against getting married?

What do you think of Veera?

Did Jaggi show courage by deciding to lodge a police complaint, or did she betray her parents?

Do you agree with her choice?

Real-life Examples

Begum Hazrat Mahal was a woman who rose from humble origins to be the queen of Nawab Wajid Ali Shah of Awadh. She was regent to her twelve-year-old son after her husband was restrained in Calcutta by the British. At a time when women were confined behind the purdah, Begum Hazrat Mahal boldly stepped forward to bring her Hindu and Muslim population together and led a courageous rebellion against the British to save the autonomy of Awadh. She even raised women's military units, commanded by a Dalit woman general, Uda Devi. Begum Hazrat Mahal herself led a military charge riding on an elephant. She refused to accept several offers of pension by the Britishers and died in exile in Kathmandu. Her extraordinary courage and boldness in fighting for independence remain exemplary.

Gauri Lankesh was a prominent journalist and

activist from Bangalore, honored with the Anna Politikovaskya award. She was known for her anti-establishment and pro-Dalit stand. She was a staunch critic of right-wing Hindutva politics, the caste system, and an advocate for freedom of the press. She stood up to various threats, underwent prosecution and conviction because of her beliefs and, was finally murdered for her boldness.

Malala Yousafzai from the Swat region of Pakistan received the Nobel Peace Prize in 2014. She advocated girls' right to education when she was only 11 years old. Going to school was prohibited by the Taliban, who held sway in her area. She sustained severe injuries after she was shot in the head as a result of her stand. But she was lucky to survive and continue with her fight against the suppression of girls' right to education.

Summing Up

Courage is the first quality that you must have for character building. You can be truthful, dependable, loyal, just, and compassionate only if you have courage. Courage does not mean being a hero. It is something that comes into play in our everyday lives in many small ways. It is a way of life. No change, achievement, or progress is possible without courage. Taking a step forward always involves some risk and, therefore, courage. The fainthearted never reach anywhere far. Unfortunately, bravery does not always involve the right action. It can be selfish, motivated, cruel, violent, and militaristic. Right thinking people are obliged to show courage to stand up for what is right and condemn what is wrong for the sake of the entire society.

7

Relationships

> Taking care of your bodies is important, but tending to your relationships is a form of self-care too.
> —Robert Waldinger

If you were to recall some happy times, what would come to your mind? Maybe a birthday celebration with your friends, a picnic with schoolmates, a family wedding, or a vacation with your parents? Most of the happy occasions that you recall are likely to include your friends and family, or people you have good relationships with.

Our mental health and feeling of wellbeing are deeply related to our relationships with our family, relatives, friends, teachers, classmates, colleagues, and neighbors. Mental health and physical health are closely related, so good relationships contribute to better physical health and productivity. On the other hand, poor interpersonal relationships can cause mental health issues like anxiety and depression and other health conditions like blood pressure, digestion problems, asthma, and heart problems, to name a few. Psychological studies have found that people with strong relationships are likely to live longer. Psychologist Sheldon Cohen established a correlation between loneliness and immune system functioning. He found that students with strong relationships were less likely to catch a common cold when exposed to the virus than those who were lonely.

Healthy and pleasant relationships are a source of happiness and motivation for us, thereby affecting our success and achievement. Forming a strong connection with our family, friends, neighborhood, and community facilitates cooperation, gives us a feeling of security, and develops a secure identity. We know that if any misfortune were to befall us, we would not be alone in facing it—there will be people to help us out and take care of us. On the other hand, social isolation can bring feelings of loneliness, low self-esteem, and anxiety.

People can be judged by the relationships they maintain and the people they relate to. A well-meaning, well-behaved, compassionate, and caring person is likely to have better relationships with others than an ill-tempered, rude, and selfish person. There is a saying that a person is known by his company. People judge a person by the kind of friends he or she has. A law-abiding, hard-working person will seek friends with similar values, whereas someone who enjoys alcohol and gambling will keep company with people of similar likes.

How to Build Strong Relationships

Family and friends are there for you when you need them, but should not be taken for granted. Relationships have to be respected and nurtured for them to last.

A caring, affectionate attitude goes a long way in building relationships while being rude or derogatory destroys them. Be sensitive to other people's feelings.

Friends are helpful and supportive. A friend in need is a friend indeed.

Relationships are built on trust. Do not mislead or lie to others. Lies are bound to be discovered sooner or later, resulting in loss of trust.

The natural urge to be selfish does not go well with building goodwill. Think about others before yourself.

Compromising is a must for lasting interactions. Relationships cannot survive if one person dominates all the time.

Forgiving each other for human mistakes is part of relationships, as is admitting your mistakes and apologizing for them. Everyone makes mistakes sometimes or the other. One must forgive and forget and move on.

Meaningful Communication is the key to good relationships. People cannot guess what others are thinking. Share your thoughts with others and listen patiently to what they have to tell you. Many youngsters stop communicating their feelings and problems to their parents, which leads to a deteriorating relationship. Communicating does not mean blaming and quarreling, but exchanging ideas with an open mind.

Respect others if you want a good relationship with them. Many youngsters have parents who are less educated and less smart than they are. They never got an opportunity to study and better themselves. Nevertheless, it does not mean that they deserve less respect. All parents deserve respect from their children, even if they are not well educated, smart, or rich. They deserve respect for giving life to their children, raising them with much care and affection, for the constant sacrifices they make to provide for and educate them. Their contributions do not become irrelevant when children grow up and become better educated than parents. A youngster who betrays his or her parent's trust cannot be expected to be sincere in other relationships in life. There will probably be some differences between parents and children as they grow up. However, they can be resolved through proper dialogue. Children must remember that parents have much more practical education through their life experiences. It is good to trust and obey them most times.

Your relationship with your teachers determines how well you learn from them. Have a respectful relationship with your teachers, who are there to give you the precious gift of knowledge. To receive this gift, you must be humble, open, and eager to learn. If you find fault with your teachers or make fun of them, who will be the loser? Remember, teachers are also human beings and cannot be perfect. They also have some shortcomings. They cannot be expected to be all-knowing either. Accept that and try to make the best of what you can learn from them for your benefit.

Teenage girls and boys are naturally attracted to each other and like to spend time together. However, they are often confused about the nature and limits of their relationship. Additionally, conservative societies frown upon the intermixing of sexes, forcing them to be friends on the sly and hide it from their family and others by lying to their parents and sometimes bunking classes. Obsessive romantic relationships often result in neglect of studies. Sexual relationships can lead to severe infections and unwanted pregnancies. Clandestine and reckless relationships may result in much stress, anxiety, and guilt, damaging your career and health. Sometimes the relationships go sour and lead to animosity, threats, and blackmail.

It is natural and healthy to have friendly relationships with both girls and boys. However, one should keep in mind that there is a proper time for close emotional and physical relationships. Intimate relationships carry much responsibility for which you may not be prepared. One needs to be mature and self-reliant before getting into a relationship.

Respect and concern should be part of your relationships with your classmates, juniors, siblings, friends, and those who serve you in different ways—the gardener, the school peon, driver of your school bus, the cleaner, and the gatekeeper.

Courtesy and politeness are the mantras to make relationships work. Many people like to say that they are good at heart but have a sharp tongue. No one can take a peek into anyone's heart. You reflect through your speech and actions. Do not try to belittle your friends even in jest. Do not pick up fights for small issues. It is the small people who have large egos.

One's family is of primary importance in anyone's life. Some people are polite to outsiders but take their own families for granted. They do not realize that others will come and go, but their family members will stand by them throughout their lives. Be there to help your parents and siblings in little ways. Do not take advantage of younger siblings or boss around them.

Many people forge relationships to get some benefit out of the other, not out of genuine affection. That is dishonesty and exploitation. There must be give-and-take in relationships. If one person is taking most of the time, and the other is giving, it is an unequal relationship that will either die soon or be unhappy and frustrating. Unfortunately, many times people exploit those who are closest to them. Students who try to get the maximum facilities and money out of their parents are exploiting them. Boys who leave all the housework to their mothers and sisters without doing their share are exploiting them.

Do you find it difficult to keep a secret? You will find it

difficult to keep a friend too. We all share personal information with our friends some time or the other. We trust our friends not to share it with anyone else. Sometimes people cannot resist the temptation of passing on the information to others for sheer entertainment. It betrays the trust of the person who confided in you. Gossiping about others is a sure way of destroying relationships.

You can depend on me!

Review your Relationships

People need to identify unhealthy and damaging relationships. Many times they find it difficult to communicate their concerns to their friends and settle for unhappy relationships. Some relationships deteriorate over time. It is helpful to communicate to fix problems and identify strategies for correcting or ending relationships. Let us look at the characteristics of healthy relationships, unhealthy relationships, and abusive relationships.

Characteristics of Healthy Relationships

People in healthy relationships:

Listen to and take their friend's feelings and ideas seriously.

Communicate openly and honestly.

Do not threaten or harm their friends physically.

Respect others.

Trust their dear ones, and earn their trust by keeping confidences.

Allow others to enjoy the activities that matter to them.

Encourage personal growth in their friends.

Accept the other's choices in life.

Characteristics of Unhealthy Relationships

People in unhealthy relationships:

Believe they have more rights than others.

Shout, threaten and bully others when they are angry.

Refuse to communicate.

Manipulate others to get what they want.

Show others down and make them feel small.

Want the best for themselves at the cost of others.

Lack respect and concern for others.

Gossiping about Relationships

Jatinder and Farida are classmates and good students. Both friends often participate together in school debates and exchange class-notes and sometimes walk back home together. Their classmates start teasing them and gossiping about them. Someone calls up Farida's parents and complains about them. She has to try and clarify her position to them that they are only good friends. Nevertheless, they are both upset and stop interacting with each other.

Questions to think about:

Was there anything wrong about Jatinder and Farida's friendship?

What do you think of the classmates who gossiped about them?

What could be the reason for someone to call up Farida's parents?

What would your reaction be if you were in Jatinder or Farida's place?

Rape

Neelam and Tony are neighbors. They like each other and sometimes go out for a drive or a movie. Tony tries to get physically close to Neelam. She refuses his advances and says that she will stop meeting him if he insists. Tony's friends advise him to force himself on her because girls do not mean it when they so no. Tony takes her to his friend's room one day, spikes her drink, and rapes her after she becomes semi-conscious. He also takes some nude photographs of her and threatens to make them viral if she reports the incident to anyone.

Questions to think about:

Do you agree that girls do not mean it when they say no?

Did Neelam make a mistake in trusting Tony and going to the room with him?

What kind of a boy is Tony?

Did Tony commit a crime?

If you were in Neelam's place, what would you do?

Smarter than Parents

Savitri is an uneducated woman with two daughters and a son. She works as a domestic helper to supplement her husband's income, who is a daily wager. Her son, Manoj, is a student of +2. He is ashamed of his parents and does not like them to come to school to attend the parent-teacher meetings. He orders his mother and sisters to do personal chores for him. He often lies to his father and takes money from him for books he does not buy. When his parents try to ask him to focus more on his studies, he retorts that they are uneducated and know nothing about education. His attitude hurts his parents.

Questions to think about:

Do you think Manoj's behavior with his parents is correct?

Do uneducated parents deserve lesser respect? What does education teach us?

How do you think Manoj's behavior affects the overall

home environment?

Do you think his relationship with his sisters is good?

Do you think this kind of attitude is common in families?

Tainted Help

Pali has to attend a wedding in the family. Her parents cannot afford to buy her a new dress. Her close friend Aliya offers to lend Pali her party dress since they are both the same size. Pali is very thankful to her friend for her generosity. She wears the dress to the wedding and forwards her pictures to Aliya. Aliya shows those pictures to several girls in the class and tells them that Pali could not afford a new dress, so she lent this dress to her. Pali gets to know of this and feels very small and ashamed. She breaks off with Aliya. Aliya then tells others that she is ungrateful and thankless.

Do you think it was nice of Aliya to offer her dress to Pali?

What was Aliya's motive in showing the pictures to other girls? Was she justified in doing so?

Do you think Pali was ungrateful in breaking off with Aliya?

Where did Aliya go wrong?

How could their relationship be mended?

Rejection

Victor is the third child of his parents. Since he is a slow student and does not perform very well in studies, his elder siblings get better grades than him. His parents often rebuke Victor for his poor performance. Sometimes his father hits him. He feels that his parents give much more importance to his siblings while neglecting him. It gives him a feeling of rejection, and he starts to lose self-confidence. He fails to clear his exam for class X. He is terrified of going home and being thrashed by his father, so he decides to run away from home. His parents are anxious and lodge a police complaint. Victor is found and brought back home.

Questions to think about:

Do you think there is a communication gap between Victor and his father?

How could either of them have tried to make their relationship better?

What would be a better way for Victor to handle his failure?

What would be a better way for his father to deal with Victor?

Have you tried to sit and discuss issues with your parents?

Summing Up

Good relationships are a significant factor in determining our overall mental and physical health.

Relationships cannot be taken for granted; they must be nurtured and sustained.

Relationships require respect and concern for the other.

Relationships require forgiveness and being non-judgemental.

Communication and honesty are essential to relationships.

Relationships can only endure if they are not exploitative.

It is vital to review relationships, identify unhealthy, and abusive relationships and correct or break them up.

8

Sexuality and Romance

> Ideologically, ignorance is no advantage when others have knowledge, especially knowledge misused, and people who know nothing of sex can take risks unknowingly and be taken advantage of.
> —Martha Cornog

The attraction between girls and boys as they step into adolescence is natural. And yet, Indian society does not look kindly upon girl-boy relationships, placing rigid behavior codes on such interactions. As a result, youngsters are often confused and frustrated about how to handle their sexual urges. To make things worse, they are not educated in the functioning of their reproductive systems or sexuality in its totality.

Sexuality is not only about having sex. Sexuality is complex and personal and involves your feelings of physical or emotional attraction towards other people and your expression of it. It is about physical intimacy, thoughts, and attitudes. It is as much about the mind as about our bodies. It also forms part of our sense of self, including our gender identity. People might have different experiences of sexuality. Each one of them has the right to choose and express it, given that it does not harm others. Sexuality is influenced by one's family, culture, religion, spirituality, laws, science, and politics.

Discussing sexuality has been taboo in our society. With few reliable sources to learn from, teenagers often grow up confused and ignorant about their bodies. They experience strong sexual urges as their bodies grow and develop, and most of them do not know how to deal with them. Very often, they are ridden by guilt or find unacceptable ways of sexual gratification.

Men and women may have a variety of sexual orientations. They may be heterosexual, homosexual, bisexual, or indeterminate. Do you know what the acronym LGBTQ stands for? The LGBTQ community has hardly been given any attention or discussed in society, so you may not have heard of them. Here are the full forms and meanings for LGBTQ:

L—Lesbians. It is a term used for women who are sexually attracted to other women instead of men.

G—Gay. Men who are sexually attracted to other men instead of women are called gay.

B—Bisexual. These are people who are attracted to both men and women.

T—Transgender. These people have a gender identity different from their given gender. Transgender men may like to dress as women, use makeup, and behave more like women. Transgender women may want to dress and act like men.

Q—Questioning. This term applies to people who do not have clear sexual inclinations and are still in the process of finding an identity.

The social condition of LGBTQ communities is pitiable. Those who are physiologically hermaphrodites are looked upon as a travesty of nature and abandoned by their parents at birth. They are adopted and brought up by communes of similar people who make a living from dancing and singing. Very few of them get education opportunities. Even fewer get a chance to find a respectable job. People from the LGBTQ groups are looked down upon by society with disdain and disgust. Social ostracization robs them of an opportunity to live normal, happy, and fulfilling lives. As a result, most of them keep trying to hide their sexual inclinations from their families, friends, and society. They grow up ridden with guilt, shame, and a feeling of inferiority for no fault of theirs. It must be understood here that there is nothing abnormal about LGBTQ people. Many parents and teachers try to counsel them to change and reform, but it is not possible to change people's inherent orientations. The LGBTQ person does not have a disease to be cured. They are naturally different and must be accepted as such. To judge anyone negatively for being born different is unfair and inhuman.

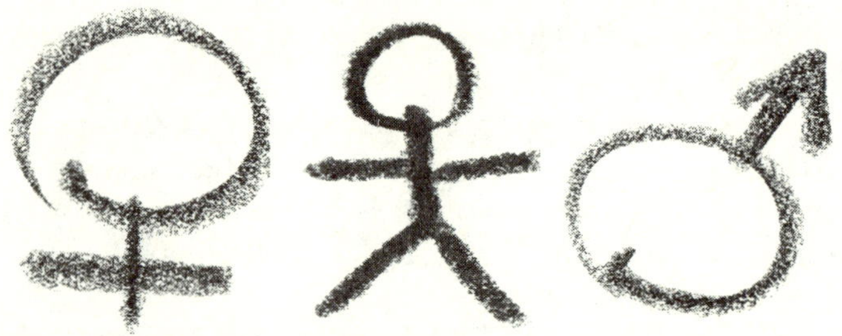

Let us look at values related to sexuality:

Sexual urges are a natural and healthy part of growing up, and you must not feel guilty about them. During puberty, the brain produces certain hormones that stimulate sex organs. These result in outer bodily development and sexual urges.

It is normal for boys and girls to feel attracted to each other after the onset of puberty. They may develop a strong attraction to someone accompanied by unreasoned passion and a sense of excitement, which is generally short-lived. It is called infatuation. As a result of watching unrealistic and obscene films, many boys think it is okay to chase and tease girls to attract their attention. These are not acceptable ways to be friends with a girl. Such actions are offensive, annoying, and unsocial. They are also disrespectful to girls. The following actions are termed as sexual harassment and can attract legal action and jail for boys:

1. Bothering a girl by following her, passing lewd remarks at her, touching or threatening her.

2. Blackmailing a girl into giving in to their demands.

3. Sending her unwelcome messages on the mobile phone or calling her up repeatedly.

4. Taking her photos or videos and circulating them on social media.

5. Hacking social media accounts of a person.

6. Posting nasty remarks about her on social media to defame her.

7. Forwarding obscene or pornographic material on phones or laptops is also punishable under law.

The last four actions are deemed to be cybercrimes and can attract a jail sentence.

Sexual relationships bring happiness only if they are established at the right age, right time, and after careful thought. Sexual relations should be based on honesty, mutual respect, and responsibility. School time is not the right time to establish sexual relationships. Teenagers are at a stage where they need to focus entirely on preparing for their careers. Relationships can be very distracting and stress-inducing. They still have many years to go before they can afford to be in a serious relationship, so it is best to wait for the right time.

Love and sex are not the same. Do not confuse the two. Many boys in a relationship coerce their girlfriends into a physical relationship in the name of love. Sexual relationships should not be misleading, coercive, or exploitative. No one should be emotionally manipulated into having a physical relationship. Some boys urge their girlfriends into a sexual relationship promising marriage. It may never materialize and can leave the girl feeling cheated and exploited. Boys can face severe punishments for rape and misleading girls to have sex based on false promises of marriage.

Sex with an underage girl (below 18 years of age) can lead to punishment even if consensual.

Having sex with a married woman is against the law and can send you to jail.

Sexuality is not only physical; it also involves emotions, psychological and ethical dimensions. All sexual decisions affect your life and have consequences that may be long-lasting. Girls must learn to take a stand and refuse casual sexual relationships for their health and self-respect.

People indulging in casual sex disrespect their bodies. Female teenagers who rush into having sex too early can pay a heavy price through unwanted pregnancies, feelings of guilt, depression, and anxiety. Irresponsible and unsafe sex can also cause sexually transmitted diseases,

social and legal problems. Boys can be legally penalized for rape, while girls can face serious health issues and social shame. Their relationship with their family also suffers.

Traditional societies have since long controlled women's sexuality. Many families still feel entitled to control who a girl meets, who she marries, and how many children she bears. It is unjust and suppressive of her rights as a free individual who must make her own decisions. These social attitudes must change.

Situation 1

Minni and Sahil are students of class XII. They are both bright students and are aiming to go for professional courses after completing school. They become emotionally involved and start meeting after school, lying to their parents for going out of the home. They often skip extra classes and tuitions to spend time together. They have long conversations on their mobiles at night, due to which they miss out on sleep. As a result, they are often sleepy in class and cannot concentrate. Their parents get suspicious and monitor their movements, leading to quarrels. Sahil threatens to leave home and go away. Their teachers are unhappy because they miss classes, and their academic performance goes down. Both of them perform poorly in the exams. Sahil fails to get admission to the professional course while Minni's father refuses to let her study further. It frustrates Minni, and she fights with Sahil, blaming him for ruining her future. They break up their relationship and end up being bitter and miserable.

Questions for you:

Was it normal for Minnie and Sahil to be attracted to

each other?

How should they have handled their relationship better?

How could they have managed their relationship with their parents in a better way?

How did their romantic relationship affect their lives?

Was Minni's father's reaction in disallowing her studies correct? Why?

Where to draw a line
in relationships?

Situation 2

Tina is a student of class X. Her parents cannot afford to buy her good clothes and luxuries, which many of her classmates enjoy. She feels very embarrassed because she has to attend school in old and shabby uniforms. She has no beautiful clothes to wear whenever her friends invite her to their birthday parties. Other girls carry trendy bags and wear nice shoes and jewelry. Tina develops an inferiority complex for the lack of all these. She keeps to herself most of the time and avoids mixing up with other girls. An older man Suraj, who is known to the family, shows a lot of interest in her. He starts giving her lifts to her school and buys her chocolates and gifts.

Tina is happy to get so much attention and gifts. Suraj persuades her to go out with him for meals. He starts giving her money next. Tina hides all this from her parents. One day he takes her to a hotel and tries to molest her. Tina knows she will stop getting gifts and money if she refuses him. She gives in to his advances, thinking that it's no big deal in return for all that she gets. It happens again and again, and she gives in every time. Eventually, the gifts and money stop coming. She realizes that she is being exploited and tells Suraj that she wants nothing more to do with him. He threatens her that he has some nude pictures of her, which he will post on social media if she does not go with him. Tina is caught in an uncomfortable position. She falls ill from catching a sexually transmitted infection. She lies to her parents and often misses school to go out with Suraj.

Questions for you:

Do you think Tina's needs were essential?

When was the right time for her to stop seeing Suraj?

Did she make a good choice in giving him sexual favors for gifts and money?

What were the risks she took in doing this?

Had you been in her place, how would you have handled the situation?

Situation 3

Nikhil is a student of class eight. He often paints his nails red and wears bangles to school. He likes to play female roles in school plays. His gestures and gait are rather feminine. He is more comfortable interacting with girls in his class rather than with boys. His classmates make fun of him and call him names, which often makes him cry. He sits alone on the last bench, keeps to himself, and eats alone in recess. His class teacher tried to counsel him to change his habits and act like a normal boy. She called up his parents to discuss his behavior. His parents told her that he often likes to dress up in girls' clothes at home. They have tried to stop him from behaving like a girl by scolding and beating him but have not been able to change him. Nikhil cannot understand why he is not considered normal. He has started staying depressed and is losing self-confidence. He even thinks of suicide. He no longer answers questions in class and has stopped participating in extracurricular activities. He has stopped communicating with his family too.

Questions for you:

What is different about Nikhil as compared to other boys? Is he abnormal?

How would you feel if you were excluded based on some personality characteristics?

Is he harming anyone or causing any damage through his behavior?

Can you voice his feelings?

How would you help him if you were his classmate?

No way to impress girls.

Attracting Girls

Gurmeet likes Seema, a girl from his neighborhood. He starts following her to school every day. She ignores him, so he asks his friend to join him and sings romantic songs to attract her attention. She continues to ignore him. Gurmeet stops her on the road by catching hold of her bike. Seema is very angry and shouts at him to let her go. He laughs and makes fun of her. Seema discusses the incident with her friend Farida, who advises her to tell her parents. Seema is afraid that her parents may stop her from going to school, so she avoids telling them. Gurmeet grows bolder and clicks her photos. He threatens her that he will photoshop these photos and put them on social media if Seema does not agree to meet him. Seema is scared that he will ruin her reputation by doing so and finally tells her mother about harassment by Gurmeet. Her mother reports him to the police. Gurmeet is arrested for eve-teasing.

Questions for you:

Did Gurmeet choose the right way to attract Seema's attention? Was he indulging in sexual harassment?

If you like someone, is it necessary for that person to love you back? If the other person does not feel the same way about you, how should you react?

Was Seema right in not telling her parents about it in the beginning?

What do you think is the best way to deal with such a problem: face it boldly, end it immediately, or avoid it? Why?

Does giving in to blackmail ever solve the problem?

Summing Up

Sexuality, though a natural instinct, is a powerful force that can cause havoc with one's life if it is not regulated and controlled.

Make your sexual choices at the right time and think of all the consequences before you do so.

Getting into physical relationships too early is distracting and likely to ruin your chances of making a good career.

It is not wrong for girls and boys to be friends so long as they observe a healthy distance and respect their own and each other's physical space.

It is unethical to use emotional blackmail, false promises, or coercion to force someone into a physical relationship.

It is unethical for girls to use sex as a way to get favors. It amounts to disrespecting and abusing your body.

Respect women. Make this world a safe place for them.

Sexual harassment and cyber-crimes are punishable by law. They can ruin your reputation and job prospects.

People belonging to LGBTQ groups are as healthy as anyone. They are not ill or abnormal. They are as capable of shining in life as anyone else and must be respected and included in society. Denying chances for self-growth and career opportunities to the LGBTQ community is inhuman and unjust. When we deprive a section of society of opportunities, it is detrimental to the growth and progress of society as a whole. Groups that are not included in the mainstream may be forced to resort to prostitution and crime to make a living.

9

Ethical Issues in Everyday Life

Rather fail with honor than succeed by fraud.
—Sophocles

It is better to deserve honors and not have them than to have them and not deserve them.
—Mark Twain

Have you sometimes wished that your parents could find more time to interact with you? The present competitive world and challenging economic conditions often force both parents to work long hours. As a result, they are generally too tired to give quality time to their growing children. With both parents working, young children are mostly on their own and exposed to the impact of social media and the internet. Unable to discern between positive and damaging influences, they indiscriminately pick up and follow harmful media content.

Peer groups play a vital role in developing moral standards of behavior. You spend much time with your friends, seeking their support, guidance, and advice. Sometimes, youngsters are more open to accepting peer group views over those of their parents. More often than not, they whet each other's choices based on getting instant gratification, thrill, and adventure without applying any ethical yardstick. Some may want to take the wiser option but are not strong enough to stand up to peer group pressure.

The reality for most youth today is immediate gratification, which outweighs the potential consequences of their choices. As they grow, they learn the value of delayed gratification. Success, or getting ahead, is most important for them, and they are ready to compromise their integrity for that. But success does not come from immediate gratification. Aspirations for success and material gains create pressures on teenagers and their parents, who have to finance their ambitions. In the race for gaining an end, the means often become irrelevant.

While there is no ultimate guide to ethics, we can take some simple steps to change our lives in a positive way. One thing is sure—there is a need for focused ethical training and awareness. Many of you struggle with ethical dilemmas because there are no guidelines or experiences to make good choices.

Additionally, peer pressure often makes it more difficult to make an independent choice. In growing from a child to an adult, people go through many confusing choices, insecurities, challenges, and the urge to prove themselves. Let's discuss some of the common issues that young adults need to address.

Self-discipline—Why take trouble to develop it?

It might be tempting to give in to immediate desires like

sleeping in late instead of exercising in the morning or spending an hour on mobile games during study time, but it will not make you a happy person in the long run. Of all the personal qualities needed to achieve success and happiness, self-discipline is the most important. It contributes to accomplishing life-goals, maintaining relationships, health, fitness, work ethics, and overall well-being. Self-discipline improves learning and performance. Studies show:

That students with a higher degree of self-discipline show better retention of knowledge and perform better.

That people with high levels of self-discipline are less stressed and find it easier to make difficult decisions. They are not easily swayed by momentary impulses or peer group pressure but make informed and rational decisions.

That measuring a person's level of self-discipline predicts success better than measuring his IQ.

Self-discipline is a quality that we have to imbibe through determination and practice. It is a learned behavior, not something that one is born with. Once you have decided on a set of ethics to live by, you need to enforce them in your daily routine, which will come through self-discipline. Let's say that your top priorities include your health and career. Working towards these goals will involve:

Observing regular sleeping hours to get adequate sleep.

Keeping up with a daily exercise routine.

Eating three balanced meals a day and cutting out on junk food.

A fixed time table for studies and following the best

study methods for optimum benefits.

Cutting down on the usage of electronic devices, especially your mobile phone.

Your self-discipline levels will predict how well you can fight temptations that will come your way in life to live a fulfilled life.

Good Manners and Etiquettes

"The rules of good manners are the traffic lights of human interaction. They make it so that we don't crash into one another in everyday behavior."—Pier Forni, author.

You may wonder how to include good manners in ethical behavior. However, they are very foundations of your values and interaction with your family, friends, and society at large. Being mindful of others' feelings and comfort in small ways will indicate whether you can make greater sacrifices for social welfare. Modesty, kindness, humility, and empathy are traits essential to good behavior.

The way you conduct yourself with others reflects the kind of person you are and, in turn, earns you respect or ridicule from those you interact with. Courteous behavior makes it easier to relate well with other people and motivates them to be kind and helpful to each other. It makes you feel confident and happy, creating an overall atmosphere of goodwill and cheer.

What should one do to be well-mannered and courteous?

Choose your words wisely when speaking to others. Be polite and respectful. Do not use harsh, insulting, or

foul language. Avoid raising your voice even if you are angry. It is bad manners to speak of bodily functions and tell crude jokes. Speaking ill of people behind their backs, making fun of someone, and indulging in malicious gossip shows a person in poor light.

It is polite to use simple courtesies like 'Please', 'Thank you', and 'Sorry'.

Be especially considerate to older people and women; offer them a seat if needed.

Hold the door open for anyone following you closely.

Offer food to others when eating together. Do not talk with your mouth full.

Use a handkerchief or your sleeve when sneezing or coughing. Avoid any company if you have the flu. You will spread infection in class or office.

Stand at a minimum distance of three feet when speaking to people you are not close too. Women find it especially uncomfortable if men come up too close when talking to them.

Request people's privacy. It is rude to ask personal questions to people you do not know closely. Curb your curiosity about their age, income, property, and relationships. Do not read other people's diaries, emails, or peek into their accounts. Being close friends with someone does not give you the right to know everything about that person. Respect their space.

Drugs

The incidence of substance abuse has shown an alarming increase in the world over. What gets the youth hooked on to drugs? Some of the factors might include:

Boredom—It might be merely out of boredom and for

the thrill of trying out a new experience.

Bonding with friends—It makes them feel more confident, or they feel a part of a group that uses drugs. They think that the consumption of alcohol and drugs makes them 'cool' and popular among friends.

Depression and stress—It might be a way of escaping depression and stress.

Peer pressure and low self-confidence—Some teenagers lack the confidence to say no and give in to peer pressure to try out drugs.

Do any of the above factors justify starting on drugs? Is it even a remedy for any problem? Consequences of drug use:

Teenagers who start experimenting with drugs are prone to develop drug dependence in later life.

Drugs cause impaired mental functioning, affecting memory, comprehension, and causing mood swings.

Drug intake has a high correlation with high-risk sexual activity and sexual exploitation. It may be due to the lowering of mental alertness and logical thinking or conscious sexual trafficking to meet high drug expenses.

Intake of drugs causes mental health disorders like depression, rage episodes, panic attacks, anxiety, and other personality disorders.

It may cause physical disorders like liver failure and other chronic diseases.

It brings about a decline in work performance.

A person under the influence of drugs loses control over motor abilities and is more likely to be involved in road accidents.

No employer will take on a drug addict. It can ruin one's career.

It is illegal for a person to possess, sell, purchase, store, or consume any narcotic drug.

Behavior Norms in Public Places

Youngsters enjoy hanging out together. However, they often fail to follow the expected behavior norms and create a public nuisance. One must take care of basic courtesies so as not to inconvenience the people around.

Drinking in parked vehicles, parks, or the roadside is punishable under the law.

Take care not to disturb others by being loud and boisterous in restaurants, shopping areas, public vehicles, and waiting rooms.

Do not trash places by throwing around empty bottles, containers, or wraps.

Do not vandalize public property in any way. Scratching your names on bus seats, on walls of public buildings, or historical monuments is a punishable offense.

If celebrating a function at home, switch off the music at 10 pm so that the neighbors are not disturbed. Similarly, Diwali crackers must be discontinued after 10 pm.

It is essential to wait in a queue to enter a public place, buy a ticket, transact in a bank, or board a train or bus. Keep a minimum distance of three feet from the person in front of you. Avoid touching or pushing people, and do not try to get ahead of those in front of you.

When shopping, wait for the salesperson to finish dealing with the customer ahead of you before engaging with him.

Always be polite when interacting with strangers you come across.

Never park your vehicle to block another vehicle.

Keep your voice down when eating in a restaurant with friends or family.

Do not speak loudly in a hospital and disturb patients.

Environmental Awareness

Our concern for the environment may have only been a responsibility earlier, but its urgency has made it a part of fundamental ethics and human morality. Saving our environment is directly linked to saving life on the globe. We flourish together or perish together. Make yourself environmentally aware and take on the responsibility of checking the misuse of resources by anyone around you. Here are some ways you can contribute to safeguarding the environment:

Avoid wasting electricity, water, petrol, paper, and food.

Recycle all that you can. Use every scrap of paper to write.

Grow plants.

Avoid burning gardening waste, or garbage.

Compost kitchen waste.

Do not litter.

Avoid using plastic. Use reusable things.

Avoid using poisonous disinfectants and repellents. Use organic ones instead.

Moral Challenges

Some of your friends use foul language because it makes them feel 'cool'. Each day, you hear words your parents would disapprove of. Your friends even use the names of God as if they were just bad words, and they call you a baby because you won't talk like them. What will you do?

Your father is a reputed surgeon, and it is his dream to make you follow in his footsteps. You have not done well in your exams, and your admission into medical school depends on your grades. Your friend offers to help you change your grades for a certain sum of money. What will you do?

It seems that just about everywhere you look—grocery stores, TV, billboards—you see pictures of women wearing revealing clothes. Many of your friends access pornographic sites on their mobiles. How healthy is it? Can it turn into an addiction?

Some of your friends have started drinking alcohol even though they are legally under-age. They seem to have great fun and mock you for not joining in. How will you deal with the situation?

You love the power you feel behind the wheel, and you want to see what it feels like to drive fast. You get your chance while driving alone in the car. The speed limit is 50, but there's no traffic on the road. What will you do?

You are tired of being pulled up by a teacher who seems biased against you. You are not a kid anymore; you deserve respect. The teacher asks you to stand up in the class. You can tell he's angry, and you know what's coming. How will you react?

Your best friend, Jeet, is involved in supplying drugs to students. The Principal summoned him for an inquiry. Afraid of being expelled from school, Jeet denies the

charge and names his classmate Samar, who has nothing to do with it. An innocent person will be unfairly suspended from school and carry a stigma that will affect his future career. You are called as a witness. What will you do, considering the effects of your testimony? Imagine yourself in Samar's place.

Radhika and Mita were in charge of a stall during the annual school fair. The sales money was kept in a box under the counter. Radhika stepped away from the booth for a few minutes. As she walked back to the stall, she saw Mita take some money out of the box and put it into her pocket. Radhika was confused about what to do. She hoped no one would notice that some of the money was missing, but it was detected when the accounts for the stall were checked. The teacher-in-charge investigated the theft of cash and was misled into holding a school sweeper responsible. Radhika remained silent. She didn't want to be known as a rat who spoke against one of the most popular girls in school.

Questions to think about:

Why was Radhika afraid of revealing Mita's name?

What could have been the consequences if she reported Mita?

By not saying what she had witnessed, was Radhika a partner in the crime?

Drug Addiction

Rit and his best friend, Tarun, go to different high schools. Since the third class they've been friends, but after Rit changed his school in 10th class, they do not meet too often. Rit comes from a humble background.

His father works hard to support Rit's education and hopes that Rit will start earning and help him look after the family.

One Saturday, Tarun, who met Rit after a long time, asked him to drive him into the nearest city as he didn't have his driving license. Rit hesitated as he'd recently got his license, and his parents had told him not to drive into the city. Nevertheless, he agreed because he did not want to annoy his friend. Tarun pulled out some hashish and persuaded Rit to try it. Rit gave in after much reluctance and tried it so as not to appear a sissy. Rit's meetings with Tarun became more frequent, and before he could realize it, he was addicted to the drug. Initially, Tarun provided free drugs to Rit but told him to buy it once he was addicted. Rit resorted to lying to his parents to get extra money to buy the drug. His performance in school and overall health declined, leading to anxiety and depression. He felt trapped and wanted to get out of this bad situation but did not know how. His father's words rang in his mind, "Always think of the consequences first when you do something."

Questions to think about:

Was Tarun really a friend to Rit or a drug peddler?

Who is responsible for Rit's addiction?

Is it a good choice to continue a friendship with someone who is into illegal activities? Why?

What would you suggest Rit do?

Friends vs. Parents

Jiya came as a transfer student to The High School. She felt somewhat lonely and was keen to join the group of elitist students. Jiya had a great relationship with her parents and trusted their advice to give it time. This elitist group invited her to a Diwali party to be held in a farmhouse outside the city. It was the perfect opportunity to break out of her loneliness and bond with them.

Her dilemma was that her parents would not let her go to this party if they knew it was to be held at a farmhouse out of town. However, Jia desperately wanted to go, and felt that it was one good opportunity for her to be a member of this popular group.

Jiya was reluctant to lie to her parents as she did not want to lose their trust.

Her friends advised her to keep quiet about the party's venue, but her mind struggled with several questions. Would it be worthwhile to hide the facts from her parents and risk having to lie? Why were they so strict with her when all the other students were allowed to go? What were the chances of her lie being discovered? On the other hand, everyone lies to his or her parents some time or the other. Perhaps they would never find out, and all her fears were in vain?

Questions to think about:

What do you think about Jiya's situation? Do you empathize with her?

What do you do when faced with a situation where there doesn't seem to be a "good choice"?

Why are her parents unwilling to send her to a farm party outside the city? What could be the risks?

What would you advise Jiya to do?

Drunk Driving

Aman went to a party with his friends, who left at ten. He was having a great time and decided to stay on longer. When he was ready to go, he found that people who could give him a ride were drunk. Aman thought about calling a friend but didn't want to impose so late at night. He didn't know the hosts. If he called his parents, he would have to listen to the same old lecture.
A friend offered to drop him on the way, though he was drunk too. Aman knew it was foolish to ride with a drunk driver, but he could think of nothing better. As far as he was concerned, he was in trouble either way. He needed to make a decision.

Questions to think about:

What will be the best choice for Aman?

Have you or anyone you know been in a situation like this? What did he/she do?

What could Aman have done to avoid landing in this situation?

What are the risks he took in riding with a drunk driver?

Copying in Exams

Vinita has prepared for the medical entrance exam for a year, and knows that this exam will decide the course of her life. She can solve all but the last question. Though Vinita has studied hard, she cannot recall the answer. The invigilator is busy on her phone, and Vinita can easily copy her neighbor's answer without being detected. Besides, she knows the answer is somewhere in her brain, so it's only fair that she should get credit for it.

Questions to think about:

Do you think Vinita is likely to copy the answer? Give a reason.

Would you lose respect for Vinita if she decides to copy the answer? Why?

How is Vinita's decision likely to affect her future?

Have you been in this situation? Would you change anything about your decision now?

Will Vinita's cheating affect her classmates too? Why?

***

After studying the chapters afore, it is reasonably clear why we need to work on developing values and ethics in ourselves. They serve to shape human conduct to be conducive to preserving the peace and well-being of society. Laws of the land govern formal transactions, but ethics are a self-regulating system to keep society secure and cordial because the law cannot always monitor individuals.

In the last decades, the rapid industrialization of the world has led to greater mobility and the disintegration of the family. This has resulted in many youngsters living away from their parents' guidance and building their own checks and balances to unlimited and unsupervised freedom. Staying in large metropolitan cities where people are impersonal and having no fear of community interference, sets some people free to behave in unethical ways. They feel it is okay to do whatever they want because they are in a city far away from their family and relatives, with no possibility of being found out. The race for material gains and freedom from censure has resulted in an erosion of ethics, impacting society with serious outcomes like loss of respect, co-operation, peace, and justice.

Let us vow to live by basic ethical norms and values that remain true and essential at all times and all places globally, across different countries, cultures, and religions. This, and only this, will ensure a better future for humanity.